MIX
Papier aus verantwortungsvollen Quellen
Paper from responsible sources
FSC® C105338

Pietro Salvo

Wearable technologies for sweat rate and conductivity sensors

Design and principles

Anchor Academic
Publishing

Salvo, Pietro: Wearable technologies for sweat rate and conductivity sensors: design and principles. Hamburg, Diplomica Verlag GmbH 2013

ISBN: 978-3-95489-037-8
Print: Anchor Academic Publishing, an Imprint of Diplomica® Verlag GmbH, Hamburg, 2013

Bibliographical Information of the German National Library:
The German National Library lists this publication in the German National Bibliography. Detailed bibliographic data can be found at: http://dnb.d-nb.de

The digital publication (eBook) of this work with the ISBN 978-3-95489-537-3 can be purchased on the general market or directly from the publisher.

Contents

Acknowledgements

To my parents, for their love and support during these years.

To Prof. D. De Rossi and Dr. F. Di Francesco for their help, support and supervision.

To Dr. D. Costanzo for his help.

To Institute of Clinical Physiology at CNR of Pisa, where the research was conducted.

To the BIOTEX partners, for their excellent work.

Preface

Wearable sensors present a new frontier in the development of monitoring techniques. They are of great importance in sectors such as sport and healthcare as they permit the continuous monitoring of physiological and biological elements such as ECG and human sweat. Until recently this could only be carried out in specialized laboratories in the presence of cumbersome and often expensive devices. Sweat monitoring sensors integrated onto textile substrates are not only part of a new field of work but they also represent the first attempt to implement such an innovative idea on a system which will be worn directly on the body. The purpose of this book is to present possible designs and technologies of low cost wearable sweat rate and conductivity sensors integrated onto a textile. The first chapter deals with a preliminary introduction on sweat production, composition, and applications of wearable devices. Second chapter describes the conductivity sensor: geometry, materials and coupling with a temperature sensor for precise measurements are discussed. This is followed by a chapter on the sweat rate sensor and the technologies employed to fabricate it. Sensors based on a) conductive yarns coated with hydrophilic polymers, b) conductive polymer fibres, c) hydrophilic polymers between conductive fabrics and d) humidity sensors are described in detail. Last chapter provides a study of sweat production in different body areas, the calibration procedure and the results after testing on human volunteers.

Pietro Salvo

Introduction

Wearable sensors are a new technology, which is rapidly spreading in the areas of sport and healthcare. This growth is mainly due to the athletes' need to have real time information regarding their physical status during training sessions and of course more importantly, a patient's need for a constant, low cost, non-invasive method of monitoring. In fact, detailed information is potentially available if close contact is ensured between the body and the sensors. One of the main advantages of this new technology is that the modified garment does not alter the normal activity of the user.

To be defined as wearable, a sensor has to:

- Be integrated onto clothing and specifically onto a textile substrate.
- Perform its tasks directly on the human body.

The first condition implies not only that the sensor has to be in direct contact with the garment but also that the textile substrate becomes a support to connect the body and the sensor.

The second condition defines an important constraint that is not always respected. The analysis of sweat is usually carried out by collecting the sample with a patch to be analyzed by another medical instrument. Our goal is to show that it is possible to measure several parameters regarding human sweat directly on the body, without the intermediation of other instruments. The data is promptly available for the user, by a wireless connection, on a PC. In fact, it is not necessary to directly connect the sensor to a PC since there are wireless connections available such as Bluetooth, which according to its latest specifications achieves a speed of 2.1 Mbits/sec up to about 100 meters with low power consumption.

Other properties are strictly related to the definition and use of wearable sensors. The garment has to retain all its properties of flexibility and washability, and so does the sensor. Moreover, there must be no discomfort so as to allow users to feel like they are wearing a normal garment and thus enable them to act normally. This freedom of movement is important if it means that users are no longer required to go to a medical or scientific laboratory in order to monitor certain parameters regarding their health.

Another desirable characteristic of wearable sensors is that they could be made on large scale, with cheap but high quality materials, and would only be of small dimensions.

Chapter 1 – Wearable sensors

1.1 BIOTEX project

The BIOTEX project is a Specific Targeted Research or Innovation Project, (STREP) which is part of the Sixth Framework Programme of the European Commission, Priority 2&3, joint call between IST (Information Society Technologies) and NMP (Nanotechnology and nanosciences, knowledge-based multifunctional materials and new production processes and devices). The consortium consists of eight partners from four countries and includes:

I. Centre Suisse d'Electronique et de Microtechnique (CSEM) in Switzerland which has a strong background in the field of micro and nanotechnology.
II. Commissariat à l'Energie Atomique (CEA) - Laboratory for Electronics & Information Technology (LETI) in France, which is skilled in developing electrochemical sensors.
III. Interdepartmental Research Center "E. Piaggio", University of Pisa, Italy, which is a leader in the field of bioengineering.
IV. National Center for Sensor Research, Dublin City University, Ireland, which is well known for its activity in the field of health science, nanotechnology and micro-systems.
V. Smartex s.r.l., Italy, a company active in the development of projects related to wearable instrumented garments.
VI. Penelope, Italy, is a leading fabric manufacturing company based not only on materials like wool and cotton but also on innovative ones like stainless steel and glass fibers.
VII. Sofileta, France, a specialist in integrated textile manufacturing.
VIII. Thuasne, France, is a producer of innovative products for the medical market and sports protection.

The kind of wearable sensors that are commonly studied in research laboratories or sold by companies mainly regard ECG, heart rate, skin temperature and resistance. None have implemented a biochemical sensing technique capable of measuring fluids such as sweat and blood. The BIOTEX project is the first attempt to move towards this goal, analyzing, in particular, human sweat.

Chemical sensors are complex systems since their reactive layer has to be exposed to the target sample in order for the reaction to occur. Thus, how to deliver the sample to the sensor is one of the most critical aspects involved.

Artifacts caused by movement and a sufficient amount of uncontaminated fluid are very important, therefore tests that can determine the behavior of the system are absolutely essential.

The final goal is to create a patch able to carry out a multi-parametric analysis of various physiological targets including:

- Sweat monitoring: sweat rate (perspiration), sweat conductivity, specific ions like Na^+, pH.
- ECG (electrocardiogram)
- Oxygen saturation of blood.

1.2 Sweat

The analysis of biological fluid underlies much of modern medicine. Blood is rich in information but there are a large number of pathologies that require frequent monitoring, sometimes for long periods or for a person's whole life. In these cases, blood sampling is too invasive for patients. It often requires long waiting times, it must be done in specialized laboratories or clinical structures, performed on an empty stomach and can cause infections.

One possible way out may be to strengthen the analysis of other biological fluids whose sampling is less invasive and which are less chemically complex. Easy-to-use, fast response sensors would allow both doctors and patients to get important information, thus improving prevention and cutting costs.

Sweat, in particular, seems very promising. It is composed of 98 per cent water and about 2 per cent is made up mainly of sodium, chloride, potassium, bicarbonates, urea, lactic acid, glucose and traces of other organic compounds.

The sodium concentration depends on the sweat rate, which while in normal conditions is about 20 mM, can reach 100 mM for higher rates [1]. Potassium ranges from 5 to 6 mM [2] while chloride is about 35 mM [3]. However, in the presence of cystic fibrosis, which affects the lungs, pancreas, liver and intestines sometimes leading to infections, poor growth or infertility, sodium concentration can increase to 200 mM [3] (see Table 1 for more details about concentrations). It should be noted that an increase in chloride is just an indication and not certain proof of the presence of cystic fibrosis. Other diseases may also be responsible, such as Addison's syndrome or a renal dysfunction.

Table 1. Sweat composition: main electrolytes and compounds.

Main components	Range of variation (mmol/l)
Sodium	20-100
Chloride	25-60
Potassium	1-15

Calcium	0.2-1.34
Magnesium	1.5-5
Urea	12-35
Lactate	10-15

pH is about 5 for low sweat rates while it reaches 6.5-7 for higher rates [1].
There are two types of sweat gland: eccrine and apocrine (Fig. 1). Eccrine glands are smaller, active from birth and produce sweat. On the other hand, apocrine glands, which have the same structure as hair follicles and sebaceous glands, are active only at puberty and they do not have any role in thermo-regulation. The dimensions of eccrine glands can be very different - some people have eccrine glands five times bigger than other people do.

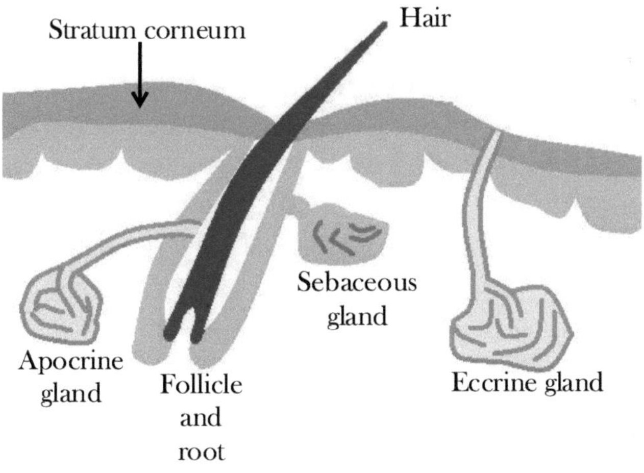

Fig. 1. Sweat glands under the skin

Together with the skin's capillary blood vessels, sweat glands regulate the temperature of the human body. In fact, the evaporation of water, which is the main component of sweat, controls the body cooling at a concentration of 0.6 cal per milliliter of evaporated sweat [4]. The body sweats when skin temperature rises over 32-34 °C. The maximum sweat rate is roughly 2 or, for a short time, 4 l/h in normal and extreme conditions, respectively.
What happens is that when the body is too warm, the flow of perspiration from the sweat glands to the ducts on the surface of the skin increases.
The two main forms of perspiration are perspiratio insensibilis and sensibilis. Perspiratio insensibilis is an incessant process caused by the diffusion of water between the derma and

epidermis. It is strictly dependant on the hydration of skin and has little relation to body thermoregulation. At 31 °C, perspiratio insensibilis has a water flux of 6-10 g/m^2·h from the skin of legs, trunk and arms; up to 100 g/m^2·h from the feet, the palms of hands and from the skin of the face.

Perspiratio sensibilis depends on the eccrine glands, which are already developed in the body from birth. Typically, on average, there are 2.6 million eccrine glands (in the skin, ranging from 1.6 to 4 million. They are unevenly distributed over the entire body with the exception of the external genital organs, lips and nipples [5][6]. They are embedded in the dermis, which is the layer of connective tissue lying under the epidermis. Their ducts penetrate the epidermis and excrete sweat.

The average eccrine glands density depends on the anatomic area. It is reported 108 glands/cm^2 on the forearm, 64 glands/cm^2 on the back, 181 glands/cm^2 on the forehead and 600-700 glands/cm^2 on the palms of hands and feet [6][7]. The maximum sweat-rate ranges from 2 to 20 nL/min/gland [8].

Sweat sampling is critical. Collection is not easy since people sweat in different ways, so there are cases where the amounts are too low. It is reported that the minimum flux has to be 1 g/m^2·min and the collection time does not have to exceed 30 minutes. Sampling methods also present some difficulties [3,9]. A typical collection procedure involves placing an absorbent material in contact with the skin from which the sweat is then drawn. This method has a critical drawback regarding the amount of sweat, which may not always be sufficient. In fact, to draw the sweat from the patch, it is necessary to make use of a vessel filled with at least 2 cc of pure water, which greatly dilutes the sample.

These considerations show that the continuous monitoring of a person may only be done by designing a system that can deliver the sweat to the sensors without being affected by any contamination or by movements of the body. In BIOTEX, the solution is to use a fabric pump that collects the sweat and delivers it to the sensors which are located directly on the fabric pump, as will be explained in detail the following chapters.

Important applications of sweat analysis include the diagnosis of cystic fibrosis, against the use of illicit drugs (e.g. cocaine) and against doping in sports, but these are not the only ones. BIOTEX applications are mainly aimed at people involved in sports, but they could also have significant advantages for obese and diabetic patients who do sports.

1.3 Applications and sensors requirements

One of the main reasons for the fast development of wearable sensors is due to their high demand in the military field e.g. helmet-mounted IR imaging systems that enhance the user's vision when visible light sensors are inadequate, and which also free the user's hands in hazardous or potentially hazardous military operations. Investment in this sector is considerably high and the interaction with other fields of application is a great opportunity for knowledge exchange. This interaction has led to the diffusion of wearable sensors in sectors like sports and clinical medicine.

An exhaustive evaluation of physiological functions may help in planning the best training program, for example deciding on the correct duration and kind of exercises that will improve an athlete's fitness and health. An opportunity to test an athlete's performance in his/her typical training environment, wherever that may be, is clearly an added value.

Sports people aim to constantly improve their athletic condition and often use several devices that provide them with information about their training session, e.g. heart rate or ECG. This is true not only for professional sportsmen and women but also for all those who like to train seriously.

Being able to monitor physiological parameters in real-time for an athlete is important in terms of their health and in order to adjust the training activity to improve performance.

During physical training, sweat evaporation is the body's most effective resource to dissipate excess heat which, otherwise, might damage the tissues and cause dysfunctions in the heart or lungs. However, an athlete must avoid dehydration since the human body needs fluids to correctly maintain normal physiological conditions.

Sweat rates depend on environmental conditions, such as temperature and relative humidity, as well as the athlete's physical condition. While there are athletes who can tolerate fluid losses of 4-5% of body mass [10], in some subjects even a 2% loss of fluid can cause a dysfunction of thermoregulation leading to a significant alteration in physical performance. The critical point is reached when the fluid deficit approaches 7% [11] of the total amount while a 10% loss can lead to heatstroke. In any case, water loss is not the only target of the BIOTEX wearable system. In fact, there are not only volume losses, but also losses of electrolytes, primarily sodium, chloride and potassium, which are lost in the sweat.

Low electrolyte levels can cause some gastrointestinal discomfort and in extreme cases, hyponatraemia, caused by low sodium concentrations in blood, which is potentially life threatening. At present, there are no wearable systems that monitor electrolyte concentrations in sweat. Moreover, wet patches that need to be analyzed in laboratories are impractical for frequent monitoring.

The usual method to quantify sweat loss is an estimation of the athletes' weight before and after exercise sessions, but this does not provide any information about the electrolyte balance.

Regarding sport, sweat analysis against doping deserves special mention. The use of illicit drugs is one of the most terrible plagues of our society. It destroys the drug-taker's health, it is a risk for people who are in contact with users, it is a source of income for criminality and governments spend considerable sums combating it. Non- invasive tests might help in the fight against illicit drugs by providing a fast and easy method to detect habitual drug users. There are several studies regarding the presence of drugs in sweat (it seems that skin is a tank for drugs) and although there is still a lot to do, in particular in developing reliable detection techniques, sweat analysis is a very promising tool to monitor habitual users of illicit drugs.

For example, if a threshold is overcome, a sound or visual alarm like a beep or a red LED may be activated. Other options are possible, like employing different sensors to monitor several health levels. If data is stored or transmitted to a PC, a specialist might provide his feedback and intervene when it is necessary (Fig. 2).

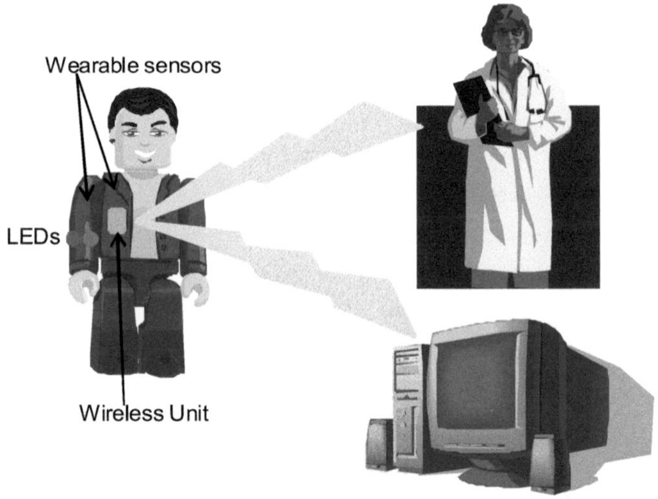

Fig. 2. Working principle of wearable sensors.

Obesity could be another strong contender for a BIOTEX application and, since it is strictly related to normal physical activity, it has many points in common with sport. It is commonly associated with an excess of body fat but it is more correctly related to a body mass index (BMI) equal or higher than 30 Kg/m^2 [12]. BMI is a statistical measurement that compares a person's weight and height, and is defined as the individual's body weight divided by the square of their height.

Obesity is often linked to hypertension, diabetes mellitus, high blood pressure, cardiovascular and neurologic dysfunctions, and also to some types of cancer.

It is caused by not only by a sedentary lifestyle and a poor diet but it is also related to genetic mechanisms, the metabolism or medicine abuse. The number of obese people is dramatically increasing in the western world and national governments have started several information campaigns to reduce its high socioeconomic impact.

Common therapies are based diets and pharmacotherapy that are specific for each patient, but which have side-effects and may only have a short period of applicability. Another option is bariatric surgery mainly based on reducing stomach size. In general, weight reduction can be accomplished, but there are operative risks (including mortality) and side effects.

All these therapies are often ineffective and the best solution is prevention, by constantly monitoring the evolution of obesity over time. An indirect analysis of a person's health from their sweat composition and production is highly relevant not only in terms of monitoring but also prevention. This is extremely important when children are obese since it is very probable they will be obese as adults. As with sports applications, a wearable sensor can help not only the patient but also the doctor to constantly monitor the patient's health status.

The third possible application regards diabetic patients [13]. Diabetes is a disorder of the metabolism. Most of the food we eat is broken down into glucose, the form of sugar in the blood. Glucose is the main source of fuel for the body.

After digestion, glucose passes into the bloodstream, where it is used by cells for growth and energy. For glucose to get into cells, insulin must be present. Insulin is a hormone produced by the pancreas, a large gland behind the stomach.

During eating, the pancreas produces insulin to move the glucose from the blood into our cells. Unfortunately, in patients affected by diabetes, the pancreas is either not capable to produce the right amount of insulin, or the cells do not respond appropriately to the insulin. Glucose builds up in the blood, overflows into the urine, and passes out of the body in the urine. Thus, the body loses its main source of fuel even though the blood contains large amounts of glucose. The two main types of diabetes are a) type 1 diabetes and b) type 2 diabetes.

Type 1 diabetes is an autoimmune disease. An autoimmune disease is when the body's system to fight infection (the immune system) turns against a part of the body. In diabetes, the immune system attacks and destroys the insulin-producing beta cells in the pancreas. The pancreas then produces little or no insulin. A person who has type 1 diabetes must take insulin daily to live.

At present, scientists do not know exactly what causes the body's immune system to attack the beta cells, but they believe that autoimmune, genetic, and environmental factors, possibly viruses, are involved. Type 1 diabetes accounts for about 5 to 10 per cent of diagnosed diabetes in the United States. It develops most often in children and young adults, but can appear at any age.

Symptoms of type 1 diabetes usually develop over a short period, although beta cell destruction can begin years earlier. Symptoms may include increased thirst and urination, constant hunger, weight loss, blurred vision, and extreme fatigue. If not diagnosed and treated with insulin, a person with type 1 diabetes can lapse into a life-threatening diabetic coma, also known as diabetic ketoacidosis.

The most common form of diabetes is type 2 diabetes. About 90 to 95 per cent of people with diabetes have type 2. This form of diabetes is most often associated with older age, obesity, family history of diabetes, previous history of gestational diabetes, physical inactivity, and certain ethnicities. About 80 per cent of people with type 2 diabetes are overweight.

Type 2 diabetes is increasingly being diagnosed in children and adolescents. However, nationally representative data on the prevalence of type 2 diabetes in youth are not available.

When type 2 diabetes is diagnosed, the pancreas is usually producing enough insulin, but for unknown reasons the body cannot use the insulin effectively, a condition called insulin resistance. After several years, insulin production decreases. The result is the same as for type 1 diabetes: glucose builds up in the blood and the body cannot make efficient use of its main source of fuel.

The symptoms of type 2 diabetes develop gradually. Their onset is not as sudden as in type 1 diabetes. Symptoms may include fatigue, frequent urination, increased thirst and hunger, weight loss, blurred vision, and the slow healing of wounds or sores. Some people have no symptoms.

All over the world, there are millions of people suffering from diabetes and it represents a substantial social and economic cost.

The fasting blood glucose test is the preferred test for diagnosing diabetes in children and non-pregnant adults. It is most reliable when done in the morning. However, a diagnosis of diabetes can be made based on any of the following test results, confirmed by retesting on a different day:

1. A blood glucose level of 126 milligrams per deciliter (mg/dL) or more after an 8-hour fast. This test is called the fasting blood glucose test.
2. A blood glucose level of 200 mg/dL or more 2 hours after drinking a beverage containing 75 grams of glucose dissolved in water. This test is called the oral glucose tolerance test (OGTT).
3. A random (taken at any time of day) blood glucose level of 200 mg/dL or more, along with the presence of diabetes symptoms.

The three previous monitoring methods are invasive since they measure the amount of insulin in the blood.

Sweat analysis can be helpful for monitoring hypoglycemic patients although what it really offers is a holistic evaluation of the unbalances in the physiological parameters that may be related to diabetes.

Knowing the applications and the targets, a wearable system should have specific electrical characteristics that can be divided into two main parts:

1. Pre-processing electronics for all the different sensors and specifically for physiological sensors. It is preferable to locate the circuitry as close as possible to the sensors.
2. A signal processing electronics responsible for data retrieving, signal multiplexing, conversion to digital, processing, and local or remote data storage. This part may be placed outside the garment for easy access, e.g. the battery and all those electronics that does not need to be washable or flexible.

This splitting renders the system more user-friendly since it is easier a) the replacement of the sensors and batteries and b) to wash the garment. The electronics, like patches, have to be as small as possible and should not be over 70 x 90 x 25 mm^3 with a weight of 150 g, including the battery.

Low circuitry cost is another important aspect. The price of the electronic patch should be as low as possible and production costs should be comparable to the cost of the interfaced sensors, i.e. about or less than € 5 per interfaced sensor. The cost of the detachable electronics is less limiting, since these devices should preferably be reusable. However, a production cost of € 200 seems acceptable for this product, taking into account the cost of stand-alone monitoring devices that do not rely on textile sensors.

In order to have a system which can be used both by specialists, such as doctors and trainers, patients and athletes, the user interface needs to be water resistant and as simple as possible, e.g. operated using a single press button.

Power consumption has to be low since the system has to work for several days.

Close contact with the skin is obtained through soft, flexible patches, which need to be disposable and removable from the garment. Furthermore, the biosensor must never interfere with the sweat analysis or cause harm to the users.

1.4 Market innovation analysis and level of innovation

The market is not only ready for the diffusion of wearable sensors but demand is also increasing. Smart fabrics and interactive textiles (SFITs) are likely to exceed \$ 640 US million by the end of 2008. Moreover, the compound annual growth rate (CAGR) was about 27% in the period 2004-2008.

According to BCC Research in 2007, the US market for smart textiles alone was worth about \$ 79 million. Sales of conductive fabric products are expected to more than double each year through 2012, when the market is expected to reach \$ 392 million.

BCC expects rapid growth in military, health care, vehicle safety and comfort applications, thus leading to a greater impact of wearable sensors in the global market for sensors. Very few products that were designed to monitor health have reached the market, but significant amounts of money are being invested in this technology. Most of the products already available were designed for use by athletes.

Lifeshirt, manufactured by Vivometrics, was designed for respiratory monitoring and other physiological signals, such as heart rate, EEG, EOG. Users have to wear a cap and a thimble in order to have their EEG/EOG and blood oxygen saturation monitored, respectively. Lifeshirt correlates and makes indirect measurements to obtain blood pressure, body temperature, periodic leg movement, and end tidal CO_2. In any case, its use is limited to research and military centres.

Sensatex, a U.S. company, is working on a Smart Textile Technology and on the SmartShirt System, which should be able to measure and/or monitor heart rate, respiration rate, body temperature, caloric burn, body fat, and UV exposure.

Wealthy is a system by Smartex, an Italian company, able to acquire physiological parameters like ECG, posture and temperature.

The most common products available are for heart monitoring by Polar, Reebok or Mio™, pedometers and pulse meters manufacture by, for example, Oregon Scientific and for diabetes monitoring such as GlucoWatch®, which shows glucose levels in blood.

The development of a wearable sensor, which can be integrated into textiles, for sweat analysis is a complete breakthrough. This book is, in fact, one of the first attempts to correlate electrophysiological data with biochemical information.

The results should provide lead to a more effective system than any other currently on the market. At present, to the best of our knowledge there is no product on the market that can perform multiple physiological measurements using a portable wireless system.

Furthermore, although there are some devices that can monitor some physiological parameters, there are no chemical wearable sensors currently available.

This point needs emphasizing since it represents the most important strength of the project, providing a new useful non-invasive instrument and technique for trainers, doctors, patients and users.

Protection, safety, health and also fashion are sectors which will be greatly influenced by wearable sensors and it is certainly not farfetched to imagine a future where our life will be regulated by these new sensors

References

[1] K. Sato, W. H. Kang, K. Saga, K. T. Sato, "*Biology of sweat glands and their disorders. I. Normal sweat gland function*," Journal of the American Academy of Dermatology, 20, pp. 537-66, 1989.

[2] K. Sato, "*Sweat induction from an isolated eccrine sweat gland*," American Journal of Physiology, 225, pp. 1147-51, 1973.

[3] C. A. Burtis, E. R. Ashwood, and D. E. Bruns, "*Tietz Fundamentals of clinical chemistry*," 6th edition, Ed. Saunders Elsevier, 2008.

[4] G. Rindi, E. Manni, "*Fisiologia umana*," vol. 2, Ed. UTET, 2001.

[5] W. Montagna, P. F. Parakkal, "*The structure and function of the skin*," 3rd Ed. New York: Academic Press, pp. 376-96, 1974.

[6] Y. Kuno, "*Human Perspiration*," Springfield, Illinois: Charles C. Thomas. Blackwell Scientific Publications: Oxford, 1956.

[7] K. Sato, "*The physiology, pharmacology and biochemistry of the eccrine sweat gland*," Reviews of Physiology, Biochemistry & Pharmacology, 79, pp. 51-131, 1977.

[8] K. Sato K., F. Sato, "*Individual variations in structure and function of human eccrine sweat gland*," American Journal of Physiology, 245(2), pp. 203-208, 1983.

[9] NCCLS/Clinical and Laboratory Standards Institute, "*Sweat testing: sample collection and quantitative analysis; approved guideline*," 2nd ed. CLSI/NCCLS Document C34-A2. Wayne, PA: Clinical and Laboratory Standards Institute, 2000.

[10] J. R. Brotherhood, "*Nutrition and sports performance*," Sports Medicine, 1, pp. 350-389, 1984.

[11] Y. Epstein, and L. E. Armstrong, "Fluid-electrolyte balance during labor and exercise: concepts and misconceptions," International Journal of Sports Nutrition and Exercise Metabolism, 9, pp. 1-12, 1999.

[12] World Health Organization, Technical report series 894, "Obesity: preventing and managing the global epidemic," 2000.

[13] NIH Publication No. 06–3873, 2006.

Chapter 2 – Sweat conductivity and temperature sensors

2.1 Definition and preliminary tests

Sweat conductivity is related to the presence of ions - mainly sodium, chloride and potassium. From Ohm's law, the resistance R is defined as

$$\mathrm{R} = \frac{\mathrm{V}}{\mathrm{I}} \quad (1.1)$$

where V is the difference of potential across a conductor and I is the current flowing through it. The reciprocal of the resistance is the electrical conductance, G, which is defined by

$$\mathrm{G} = \frac{1}{\mathrm{R}} \quad (1.2)$$

The electrical conductance of material of length *l* and cross-sectional area *A* is given by:

$$\mathrm{G} = k\frac{\mathrm{A}}{\mathrm{l}} \quad (1.3)$$

For an electrolyte solution, *k* is called the electrolytic conductivity and it is usually measured in Siemens/centimeters [S/cm]. The quotient *l/A* is called the *cell constant* and it depends on the geometry of the cell containing the electrolytic solution. There is another important quantity for conductivity in the literature, molar conductivity, Λ, [$\mathrm{S \cdot cm^2/mol}$], which is related to *k* by the following relationship:

$$\Lambda = \frac{k}{c} \quad (1.4)$$

where *c* is the molar concentration of the solution. When referring molar conductivity to concentration, the fact that it decreases very slightly for strong electrolytes when *c* increases needs to be taken into account. This effect is due to the decrease in ionic velocity with increasing concentrations because of the growth of the interaction between opposite ions. Two effects are pronounced in the strong electrolytes [Debye-Hückel Theory]:

1. Asymmetric effect.
   Ion motion decreases when a potential difference is applied, because of the interaction of opposite solute ions in proximity.
2. Electrophoretic effect.

Ion motion decreases when a potential difference is applied, because of the interaction of opposite solvent ions in proximity.

For the sweat of healthy subjects, the literature reports a range of values from 2 to 11 mS/cm [1], with an average conductivity of 5 mS/cm. Conductivity in aqueous solutions is also temperature dependant and a small variation in temperature significantly changes conductivity. This dependence is usually expressed as per cent per degree Celsius and it is the slope of the straight line representing the relationship between conductivity and temperature. Concentrated salt solutions, acids and alkali solutions have slopes of about 1.5% per °C.

We carried out preliminary tests using NaCl solutions, with different concentrations, in order to simulate human sweat. The choice of Na^+ and Cl^- depends on the fact that these ions have a higher concentration compared to the other ions that are in the human sweat.

The measurement was performed by placing two electrodes in the solutions and the validity was double checked by a commercial instrument (Dionex CDM1) and by impedance measurements made by using a certified cell (Metrohm, Switzerland, cell constant 0.78 cm^{-1}). A standard solution (Hanna Instruments, 84 µS) was also used as a further control.

In addition, the polarization effect was also taken into account. If a DC voltage is applied to an electrode pair dipped in a conductive solution, a double layer forms at the electrode-solution interface, which leads to the wrong results. Such a layer may include bubbles of hydrogen, oxygen or other chemical species if ions undergo a redox process.

For these reasons, an AC voltage, which constantly reverses the electrolytic effect thus preventing polarization, is used to measure the conductivity of solutions. For the tests, a LCR Meter (Agilent E4980A) was used. A dependence of conductivity on temperature was found accounting for a variation of 1.6 %/°C (Fig. 3).

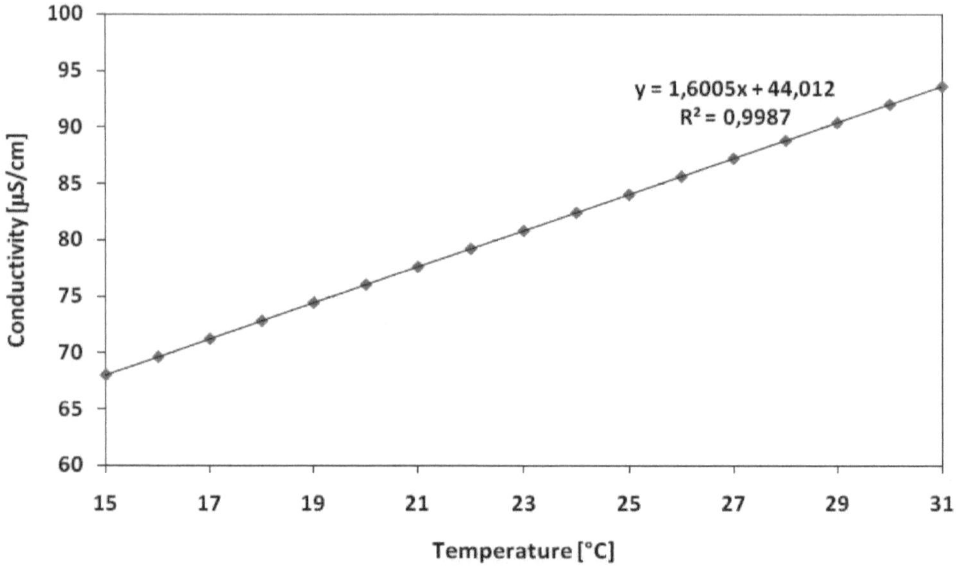

Fig. 3. Dependence of conductivity on temperature in a NaCl (0.046M) test solution.

Conductivity is closely related to the frequency-dependent electrolyte friction. Debye and Falkenhagen's study [2] was one of the earliest on the frequency-dependent electrolyte friction and conductivity. These authors considered the dynamic effect of ion atmosphere relaxation on the motion of an ion. When an ion moves in an electrolyte solution, the atmosphere cannot immediately follow the motion of the central ion and becomes asymmetric thus causing a retarding effect on the motion of the ion. In the presence of an oscillating field, the central ion oscillates and the ion atmosphere has less time to relax and remains less asymmetric. As a result, the effects of the asymmetry on the ion atmosphere are reduced and this leads to a reduction in electrolyte friction and an enhancement of conductivity at a low frequency. At a high frequency, the conductivity decreases because the ions oscillate so fast that the net ionic motion along a particular direction is smaller than when in the presence of a static or low frequency field.

To verify the dependence of conductivity on concentrations at different frequencies, a set of tests was performed. The results are shown in Fig. 4.

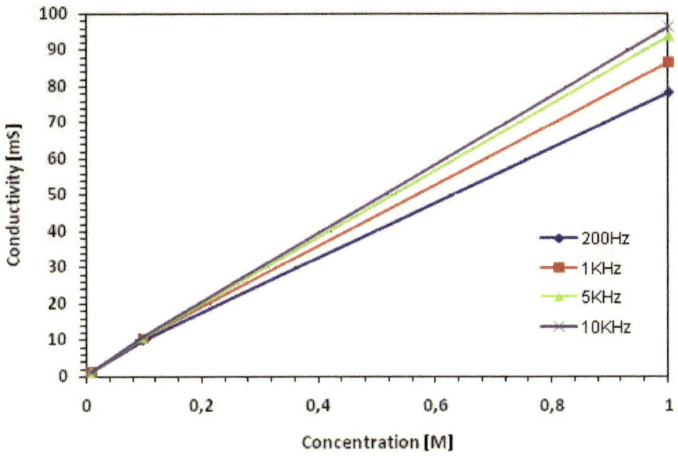

Fig. 4. NaCl solutions, conductivity dependence on concentrations at different frequencies.

Fig. 5 shows the dependence on frequency of the solution simulating average human sweat, NaCl 0.046 M.

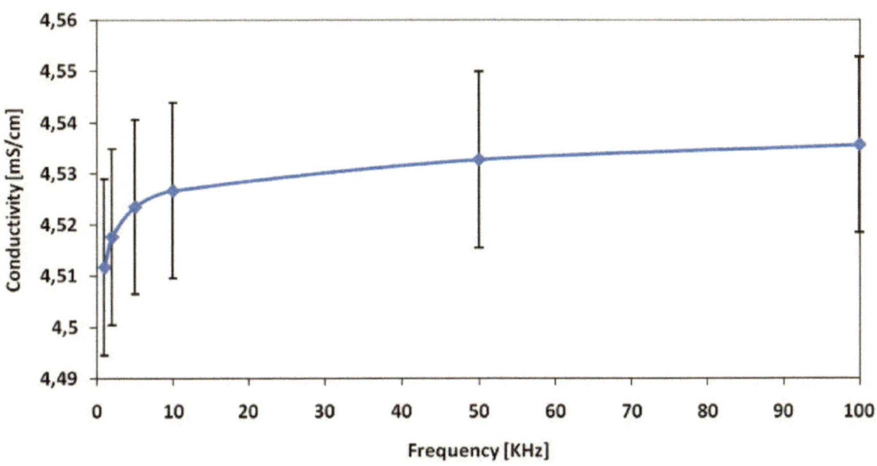

Fig. 5. Conductivity dependence on the frequency of the test solution simulating human sweat.
Standard deviation is reported as error bars.

This test proves that the variation in frequency is really small at low frequencies, thus frequency is not a critical parameter and may be chosen on the basis of considerations concerning the electronics (low power consumption, simple circuits etc.).

2.2 Geometry and substrate of electrodes

For the collection of the sweat, DCU developed a passive fabric pump, which transports the fluid through its structure to the sensors. The sweat sample is collected by a hydrophilic layer which lies below a hydrophobic layer; then goes, through an opening in the hydrophobic layer, to the top layer that has a pre-defined hydrophilic channel attached onto a piece of hydrophobic material. The channel is connected to an absorbent that will continuously draw the liquid along the channel from the skin's surface. The sensors are kept in contact with the channel, thus establishing real-time sensing between the sensor and the sweat.

After preliminary tests to determine the behavior and the suitability of NaCl simulating solutions, we chose the electrodes that we believed would be the most suitable. Flexible support needs to be wearable and the body movement must not invalidate the measurement. Furthermore, the geometry and dimensions of the electrodes need to be compatible with a resistance value easily readable by electronics in order to simplify electrical schematics. Preliminary tests were carried out using silicon and kapton® substrate sensors. Fig. 6 shows a scheme of the silicon substrate sensor.

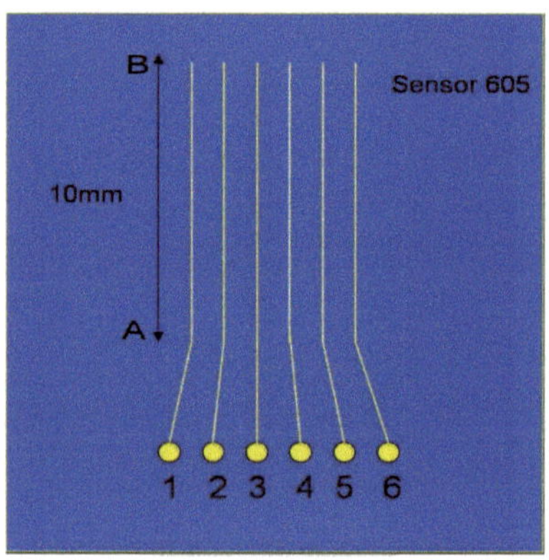

Fig. 6. Silicon substrate sensor 605.

This type of sensor, called 605, has 6 gold electrodes, with a 5 μm gap between each one, to test the conductivity at different cell constants. The thickness of each gold electrode is 0.4 μm, while the width is 100μm. A sensor, called 610, with a 10 μm gap, was also tested.

A drop was deposited at the end of the electrodes onto a small area of about 3mm in length. Fig. 7 shows the kapton® substrate sensor with gold electrodes. The distance between the 2 electrodes is 100 μm, their length and width are respectively 5 mm and 0.1 mm, with a thickness of 20 μm.

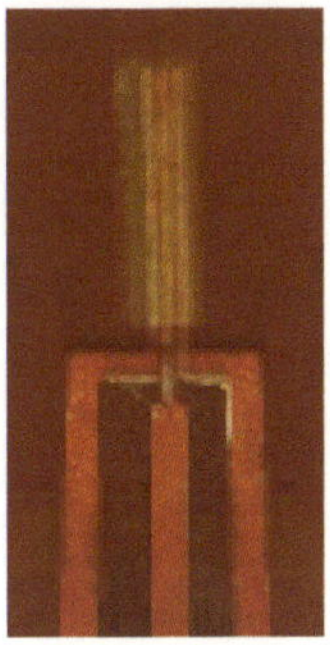

Fig. 7. Gold electrodes on kapton®.

Kapton® is a polyamide film with excellent properties for wearable sensors. It is suitable for flexible printed circuits, stable in a wide range of temperatures (from -269 °C to +400 °C), and is a good insulator.

Unfortunately, the results showed random errors in the expected values of conductivity. The explanation could depend either on the dimensions of the electrodes or on the gap between them. To investigate this phenomenon, electrodes with different geometries and gaps were set up on a kapton® printed board, always bearing in mind that the integration of the sensor in a wearable patch needs as small a final occupied area as possible. Many configurations were tested, some of which are shown in Fig. 8.

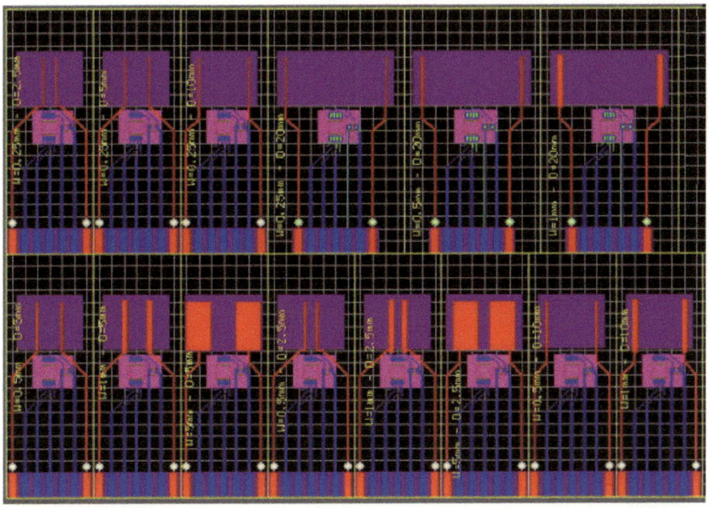

Fig. 8. Kapton® test printed board (W= width of the electrode [mm], D=distance between electrodes [mm]).

The violet area represents the active area, while the pale pink zone is where a temperature sensor has been placed to check the conductivity variations depending on temperature changes. ADT7301 by Analog Devices was chosen for its good performance and will be discussed later.

At the bottom of each sensor there are six connectors (in blue): four are for the temperature sensor and are placed on the opposite side of the electrodes while the two connectors of the electrodes are on both sides (two vias, the white circles in Fig. 8, were used).

The board is covered, both on the top and bottom, with a layer of kapton® except for the violet, pale pink and connector areas.

To cover the spectrum of the conductivity of human sweat, six NaCl solutions were used: 2, 3.5, 5, 7.5, 10 and 15 mS. Measurements were repeated at least six times. and the results, at 1KHz, 10KHz and 50 KHz which seem to be a good compromise, in the span of possible frequencies (higher frequency, which would require more complicated electronics were not justified from the results of previous experiments). This was done in order to verify which is the most appropriate for the development of future electronics.

There were two electrodes geometries that returned the best results. The first had width, W, equal to 1mm and distance, D, between electrodes equal to 5mm.

The second one, with W=0. 5 mm and D=2.5 mm, had a similar performance and was chosen because of its smaller dimension. The length was 7.36 mm.

Tables 2, 3 and 4, together with Figs. 9, 10 and 11, show the mean values of six repeated measurements with standard deviations that were made for each of the three frequencies 1, 10 and 50 KHz.

Table 2. Test results at 1 KHz.

Set	Resistance: mean value [KΩ]	Standard Deviation	Standard Deviation (%)
1	1.17	0.06	0.005
2	0.71	0.02	0.003
3	0.52	0.03	0.006
4	0.4	0.03	0.01
5	0.29	0.01	0.003
6	0.21	0.01	0.005

Table 3. Test results at 10 KHz.

Set	Resistance: mean value [KΩ]	Standard Deviation	Standard Deviation (%)
1	1.07	0.04	0.004
2	0.61	0.02	0.003
3	0.45	0.03	0.01
4	0.34	0.03	0.01
5	0.24	0.01	0.004
6	0.17	0.01	0.006

Table 4. Test results at 50 KHz.

Set	Resistance: mean value [KΩ]	Standard Deviation	Standard Deviation (%)
1	1.03	0.02	0.002
2	0.6	0.01	0.002
3	0.43	0.03	0.01
4	0.31	0.03	0.01
5	0.225	0.005	0.002
6	0.16	0.01	0.01

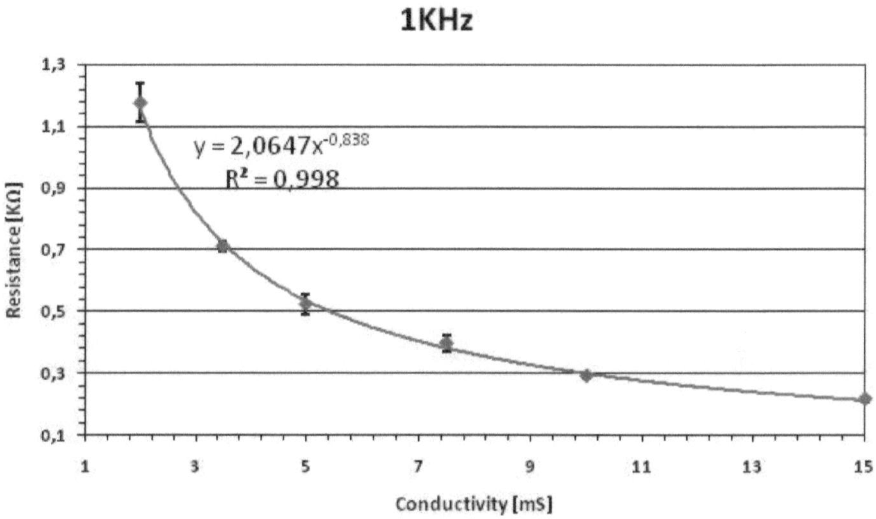

Fig. 9. Test results at 1 KHz.

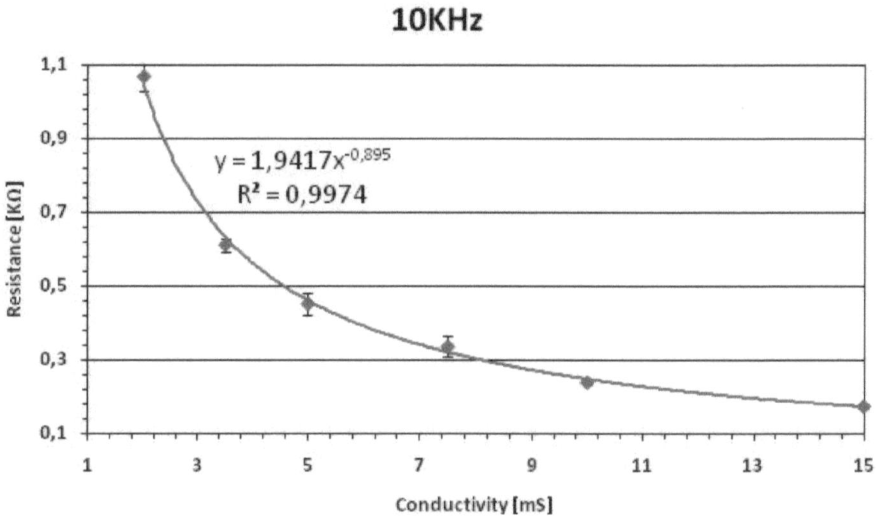

Fig. 3. Test results at 10 KHz.

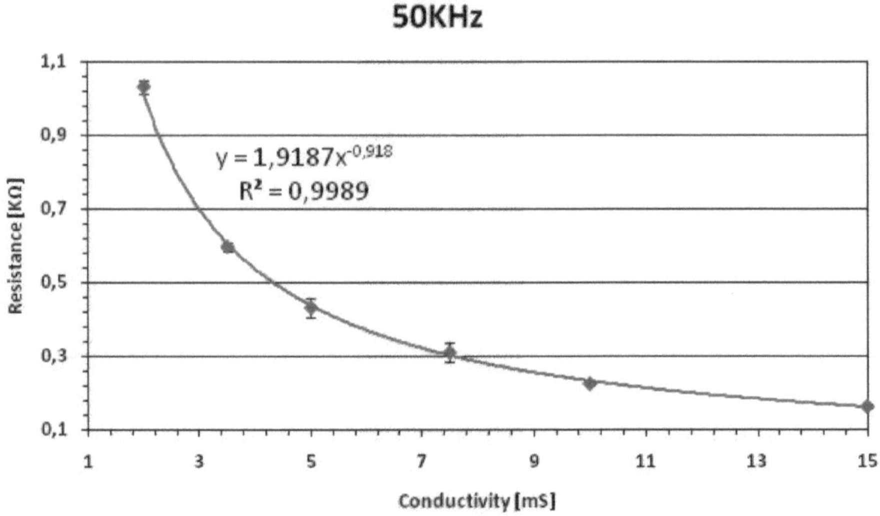

Fig. 4. Test results at 50 KHz.

The selected electrodes performed excellently at the three frequencies. In fact, from (1.3) and (1.4), we have:

$$k \cdot \mathrm{R} = \frac{l}{A} = cell\ constant \quad (1.5)$$

This formula is also confirmed by the goodness of the fits reported Fig. 12 (Fits form Figs. 11 and 12 have similar results). In Matlab, data were fitted with the hyperbolic equation $x \cdot y = a =$constant. The result was the equation $\mathrm{R} \cdot k = 2.372$, coefficients $R^2 = 0.9733$ and RMSE=0.055, which is an excellent approximation of a hyperbola.

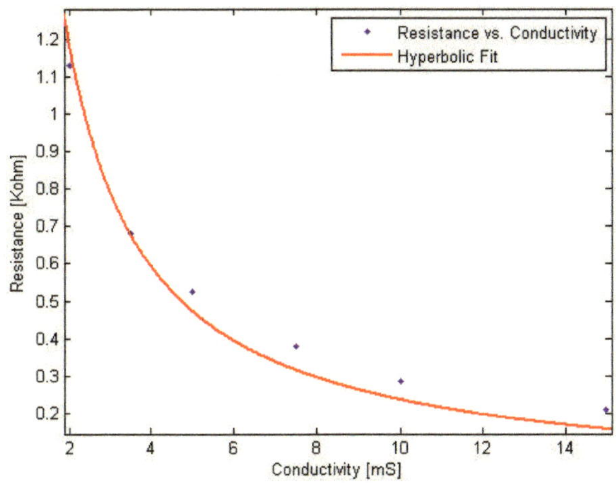

Fig. 5. Hyperbolic fit (x·y=constant) of test results at 1KHz.

Since it was again proved that the test frequency had a negligible effect on the results and considering that a low frequency simplifies the design, improves performances and lowers the cost of electronic measurements, 1 KHz was chosen.

2.3 Temperature sensor

Although the introduction of a temperature sensor was not initially planned for in the BIOTEX project, what we said in Section 2.1 in terms of the effect of temperature on conductivity and the need for a temperature correction of the data produced by the Na^+ sensor developed by CEA led to a change in the initial plans. The chosen sensor was thus the ADT7301 by Analog Devices, whose most important characteristics are:

a) Dimensions: 3 mm x 4.90 mm x 1.5 mm.
b) Operating temperature range: −40 °C to +150 °C.
c) Accuracy: ±0.5 °C (typical).
d) Resolution: 0.03125 °C.
e) Thermal Time Constant: 2 sec. The thermal time constant is the time it takes for a temperature delta to change to 63.2% of its final value. For example, if the ADT7301 experiences a thermal shock from 0 °C to 100 °C, it would typically take two seconds for the ADT7301 to reach 63.2 °C.

Since ADT7301 is not waterproof, it could not be put directly in contact with a conductive solution like sweat.

The idea was to avoid putting the temperature sensor on the same side of the conductive sensor, but instead to put it on the other side of kapton®.

The sensor is made up of 3 kapton® layers whose total thickness is less than 1mm. The two external layers, which just act as covers for the non-sensing part of the sensor, are 20 μm thick. Hence, a rectangular hole was made in the middle layer and in one of the cover layers with the same size as the temperature sensor. Thus, the remaining 20 μm of the kapton® would protect the ADT7301 from sweat and hopefully, at the same time because of the small thickness of this kapton® layer, it would not alter the accuracy of the temperature sensor.

Because kapton® is a good insulator, we had to prove that the 20 μm layer does not alter the accuracy of the temperature sensor). The sensor was tested by creating an adiabatic chamber where two copper blocks were maintained at different temperatures.

The ADT7301 was positioned between the two blocks. A simplified diagram is shown in Fig. 13.

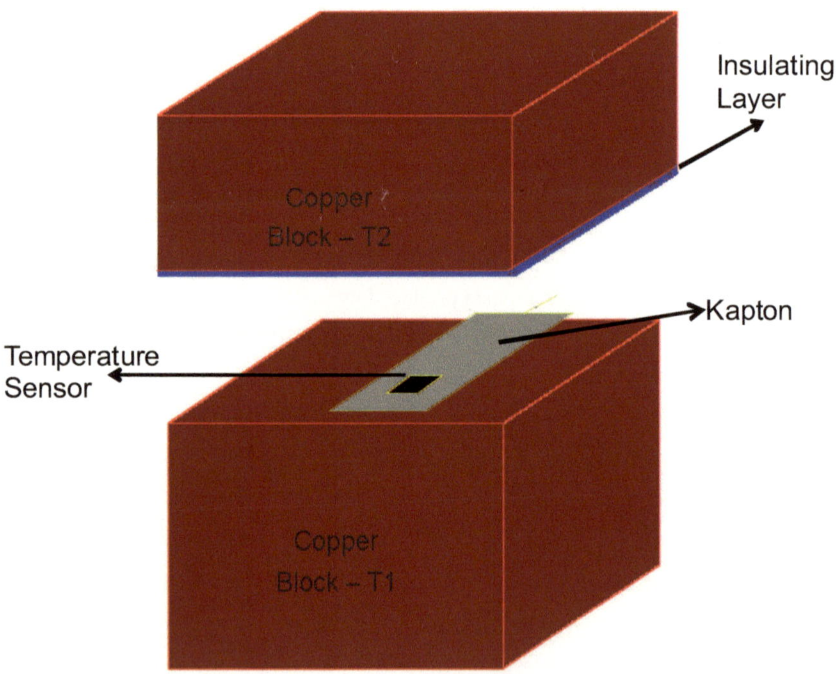

Fig. 6. The temperature testing system.

The aim of this system is to prove that the ADT7301 returns the temperature T1, representing the temperature of the sweat in the fabric pump, without being sensitive to T2, representing the temperature of the external environment.
In each block there is a thermocouple PT-100 probe connected to a digital multimetre (Mod. 2700, Keithley Instruments) to read the temperature while a resistor is inserted into the first block and is controlled by a power unit, which allows T1 to be modified.
To isolate the sensor from the upper block, three materials were tested: a mylar® layer, a neoprene layer and a polyurethane glue. Mylar® is a polyester film known for its thermal stability which has a thermal conductivity of $8.05 \cdot 10^{-4}$ W/cm·K at 27 °C and a density of 1.4 g/cc.
Neoprene® is a synthetic rubber which has a thermal conductivity of $3.8 \cdot 10^{-4}$ W/cm·K for a sheet of 126 mm. This means that the thermal resistance may be greatly increased by adopting a thinner sheet: 1cm in our case.
Polyurethane is an organic polymer whose sheets have a thermal conductivity of $\sim 2.3 \cdot 10^{-4}$ W/cm·K at 27 °C.
Figs. 14, 15 and 16 show the effects of Mylar®, Polyurethane glue and Neoprene®. The temperature card reader was only able to detect temperature variations of 0.5 °C.
The first two materials tested did not manage to insulate the ADT7301. The graphs highlight the gap between T1 and T (ADT7301). In addition, we also expected T2 to increase very slowly from its starting value (we expected the insulator to stop the heat transfer from block T1 to T2). However this hypothesis proved false in these two cases as the temperature sensor returned a value which was close to the mean of T1 and T2. The Neoprene® layer, on the other hand, proved to be an excellent insulator and the sensor perfectly followed the temperature increment. When the temperature decreased, the sensor seemed to show a slow response but this may be explained by analyzing the system. The lower block is a 6x6x6 cm copper cube, thus it has a high thermal capacitance. Furthermore, the adiabatic chamber causes a very slow decrease in T1. Considering that the reading of the sensor was only able to show variations of 0.5 °C, it is clear that it was not the sensor that was slow but the copper block which slowly decreased its temperature.

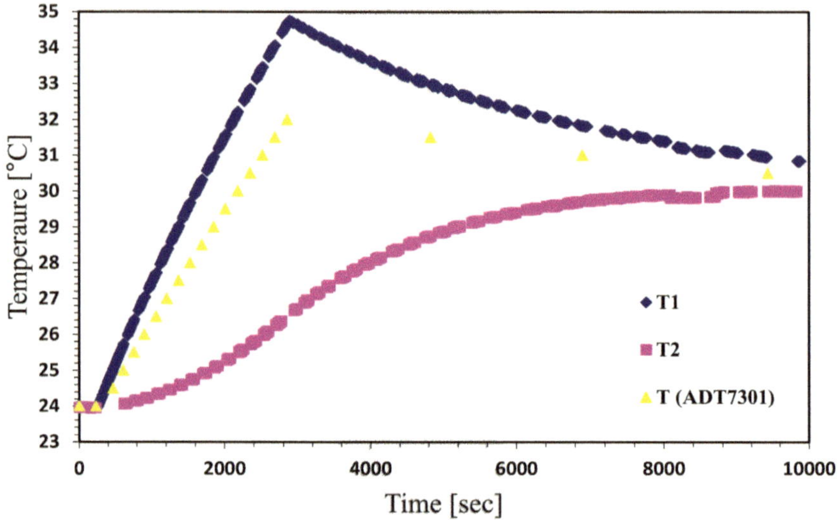

Fig. 14. Temperatures of ADT7301, BlockT1 and BlockT2 with Mylar® layer as an insulator.

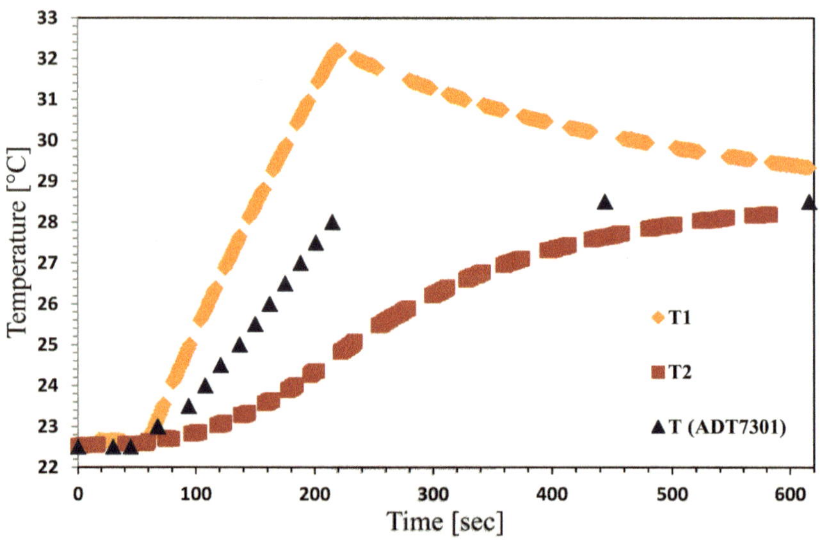

Fig. 15. Temperatures of ADT7301, BlockT1 and BlockT2 with Polyurethane glue as an insulator.

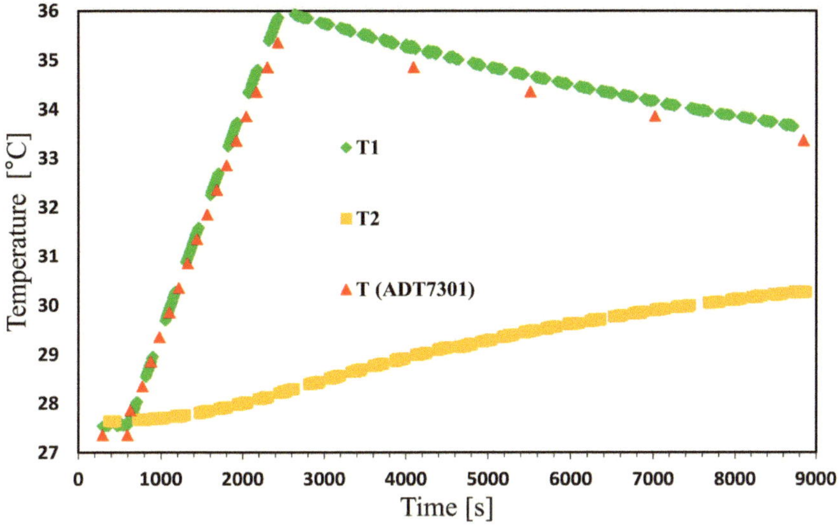

Fig. 7. Temperatures of ADT7301, BlockT1 and BlockT2 with Neoprene® layer as an insulator.

The last tests involved the possible difference in temperature when placing the ADT7301 directly in contact with the fabric pump channel or separating it by using the thin kapton® layer.

The order of these two tests was:

1) Block 1 (heated) - temperature sensor - kapton® layer - neoprene® layer (thermal insulator) - block 2.
2) Block 1 (heated) - kapton® layer - temperature sensor - neoprene® layer (thermal insulator) - block 2.

The two graphs in Fig. 17 show that there is no substantial difference if the sensor is placed in direct contact with the heated block or on the other side.

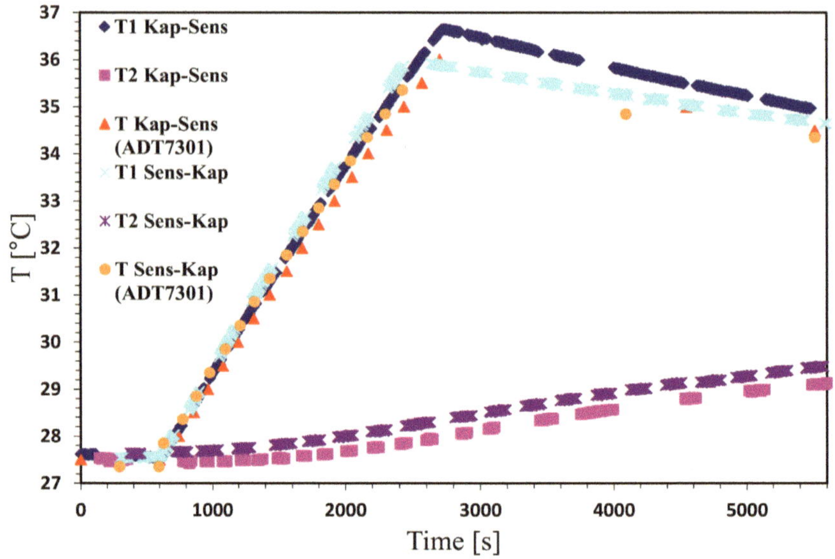

Fig. 8. Difference between placing the ADT77301 on the fabric pump channel (Sens-Kap) or on kapton® (Kap-Sens).

Comparing the two cases, it should also be remembered that the ADT7301 is 1.5 mm thick which represents another obstacle when placing it directly on the fabric channel pump. In fact, this thickness could cause an imperfect adhesion of the other sensors on the channel. The effect of which would be to prevent contact with the sweat. Therefore, separating the temperature sensor from the channel of the pump by just a 20 μm layer turned out not only to be a good idea but also essential for the sensor to be operated correctly. This greatly simplified the design of the multi-parametric patch, which includes conductivity, temperature and Na^+ sensors.

2.4 Conductivity and temperature sensors

Schematics of the multi-parametric patch are shown in Fig. 18.

Dimensions

A: 50.4 mm

B: 18.4 mm

C: 10.4 mm

D: 7.6 mm

E: 20.4 mm

Sensors

1. Sodium (Na^+)
2. Conductivity
3. Temperature

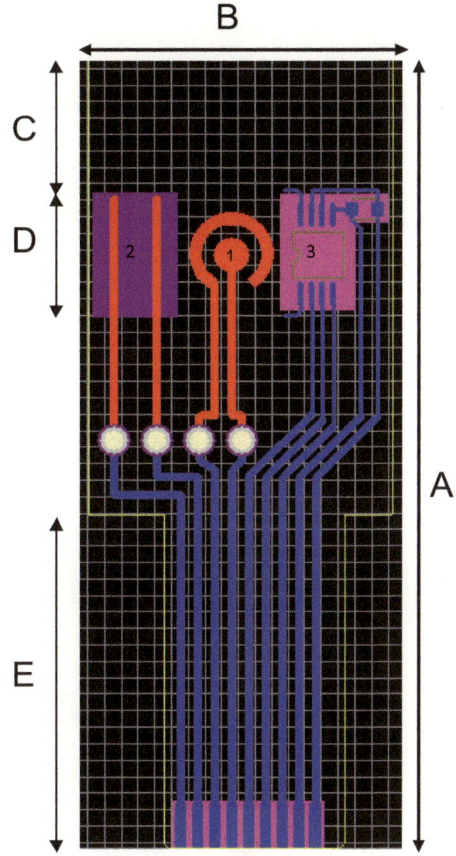

Fig. 18. Conductivity, temperature and Na+ sensors on kapton®.

C and E are are so long because they are the areas where the patch is glued onto the fabric. Sensor patch is shown in Fig. 19 while its placement on a fabric pump is shown in Fig. 20. A multi-parametric waistband is used to hold patch in place.

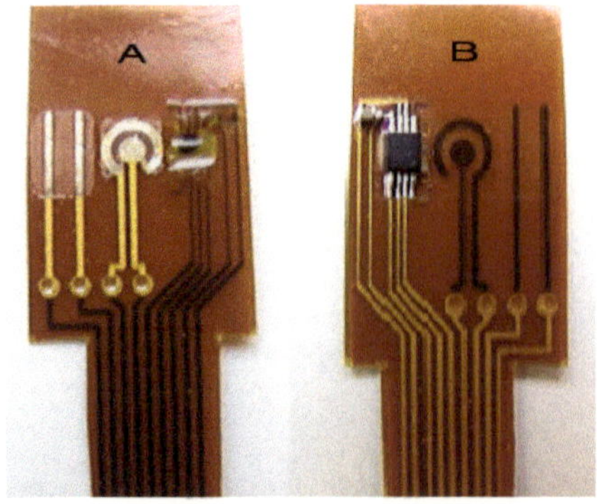

Fig. 9. Multi-parametric patch: A) Conductivity and Na^{+} sensors, B) ADT7301. The Na^{+} sensor is based on the design made by CEA-LETI.

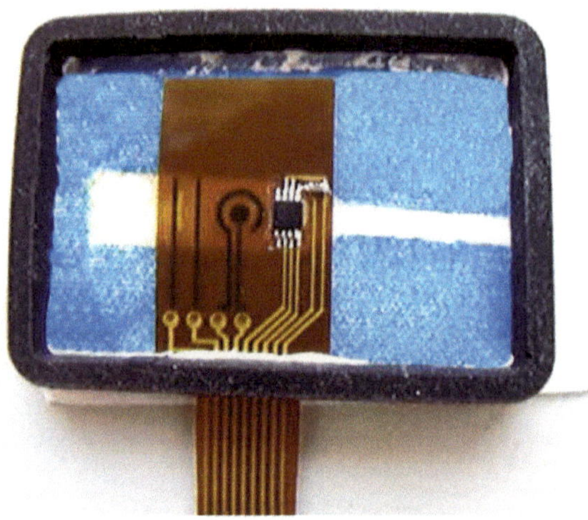

Fig. 10. Multi-parametric patch on fabric pump. The fabric pump is made by DCU.

References

[1] N. P. Lundgren, N. L. Ranianathan, A. S. Gupta, and H. S. Chakravarti, "*Electrical conductivity and specific gravity of small volumes of human sweat and their relations to the salt concentration,*" Indian Journal of Medical Research, 43(1), pp. 157-164, 1955.

[2] P. Debye and H. Falkenhagen, "*Dispersion of the Conductivity and Dielectric Constants of Strong Electrolytes*," Phys. Z., 29, pp. 121–132, pp. 401–426, 1928.

Chapter 3 - Sweat rate sensor

3.1 Measurement of flow

Sweat rate is defined as the flow of water vapor emitted by the skin, i.e. the amount of water emitted per unit area during a defined period of time. For adults the literature reports an average sweat loss of about 500-700 ml/day in mild climate conditions (T=25 °C, Relative Humidity RH=50%), but the excretion of about one liter of sweat in 15 minutes is also possible in extreme conditions (e.g. in saunas).

An estimation of sweat rate can be calculated by taking an average body surface area (BSA) of 1.7 m^2, in about 10-17 $g/m^2 \cdot h$ in mild climate conditions and about 2300 $g/m^2 \cdot h$ in extreme conditions. There are several formulas to estimate BSA e.g. the Mosteller formula [1]:

$$\mathrm{BSA}\ [\mathrm{m}^2] = \sqrt{\frac{weight\ [\mathrm{Kg}] \cdot height\ [\mathrm{cm}]}{3600}}$$

or the DuBois and DuBois formula [2]:

$$\mathrm{BSA}\ [\mathrm{m}^2] = \frac{weight\ [\mathrm{Kg}]^{0.425} \cdot height\ [\mathrm{cm}]^{0.725}}{139.2}$$

The skin is a complex structure, but a homogenous skin model is often assumed to allow the application of Fick's first law of diffusion to analyze the sweat rate. Fick's first law postulates that the flow goes from regions of high concentration to regions of low concentration. Therefore, the flow is proportional to the concentration gradient and depends on spatial position. In one dimension, the first law is:

$$\mathrm{J} = -\mathrm{D}\frac{\partial \mathrm{C}}{\partial x} \quad (1.5)$$

where

- J is the diffusion flow [$mol/m^2 \cdot s$];
- D is the diffusion coefficient [m^2/s];

C is concentration [mol/m^3];

- x is the position in one-dimensional space [m].

For water vapor and at 25°C, D is $2.49 \cdot 10^{-5}$ m^2/s and increases by about 0.7% per degree.

A continuous measurement of the sweat rate is rather difficult due to the low flow of water involved and the need for the sensor to be integrated into a fabric.

The evaporation of water from any surface establishes a water-vapor concentration gradient. [3] Nilsson had the idea of using an open cylindrical chamber to measure relative humidity (i.e. water concentration) at two points of a probe placed on the skin. A quantity proportional to the difference in water-vapor concentration could then be derived by (1.5). Although the probe was not suitable for a wearable device because of its large dimensions, the measurement principle was adopted to create a sweat rate sensor. The sweat rate sensor is made up of two humidity sensors inserted into a fabric patch at different heights and separated by a membrane or a fabric net. The first R.H. sensor is kept close to the skin while the second is nearer the external environment.

3.2 Humidity sensors

The most important specifications to bear in mind when selecting a humidity sensor are [4]:

1. Accuracy
2. Repeatability
3. Long-term stability
4. Ability to recover from condensation
5. Resistance to chemical and physical contaminants
6. Size
7. Packaging
8. Cost effectiveness.

Additional significant long-term factors are the costs associated with sensor replacement, field and in-house calibrations, and the complexity and reliability of the signal conditioning and data acquisition circuitry.
Humidity sensors can be grouped into three categories:

1. Resistive humidity sensors.
2. Thermal conductivity humidity sensors.
3. Capacitive humidity sensors.

3.2.1 Resistive humidity sensors

Resistive humidity sensors measure the change in electrical impedance of a hygroscopic medium such as a conductive polymer, salt, or treated substrate. The impedance change is typically an inverse exponential relationship (non-linear) to humidity. Resistive sensors usually consist of noble metal electrodes either deposited on a substrate using photoresist techniques or wire-wound electrodes on a plastic or glass cylinder. The substrate is coated with salt or a conductive polymer.

When it is dissolved or suspended in a liquid binder it functions as a vehicle to evenly coat the sensor. Alternatively, the substrate may be treated with activating chemicals such as acid. The sensor absorbs the water vapor and ionic functional groups are dissociated, resulting in an increase in electrical conductivity. The response time for most resistive sensors ranges from 10 to 30 s for a 63% step change. The impedance range of typical resistive elements varies from 1 kΩ to 100 MΩ. Most resistive sensors use a symmetrical AC excitation voltage with no DC bias to prevent polarization of the sensor. The resulting current flow is converted and rectified to a DC voltage signal for additional scaling, amplification, linearization, or A/D conversion.

The "resistive" sensor is not purely resistive as capacitive effects >10–100 MΩ make the response an impedance measurement. The drawbacks of some resistive sensors involve their tendency to shift values when exposed to condensation if a water-soluble coating is used and premature failure when exposed to chemical vapors. Furthermore, they have significant temperature dependencies when installed in an environment with large (>12 °C) temperature fluctuations. Simultaneous temperature compensation is incorporated for accuracy. The small size, low cost, interchangeability, and long-term stability make these resistive sensors suitable for use in control and display products for industrial, commercial, and residential applications.

3.2.2 Thermal conductivity humidity sensors

Thermal conductivity sensors measure absolute humidity by quantifying the difference between the thermal conductivity of dry air and that of air containing water vapor. They consist of two matched negative temperature coefficient (NTC) thermistor elements in a bridge circuit. One is hermetically encapsulated in dry nitrogen and the other is exposed to the environment. When current is passed through the thermistors, resistive heating increases their temperature to >200 °C. The heat dissipated from the sealed thermistor is greater than the exposed thermistor due to the difference in the thermal conductivity of the water vapor compared to dry nitrogen. Since the dissipated heat yields different operating temperatures, the difference in resistance of the thermistors is proportional to the absolute humidity.

A simple resistor network provides results in the range of 0–130 g/m^3 at 60 °C. The typical accuracy of an absolute humidity sensor is +3 g/m^3 which converts to about ±5% RH at 40 °C and ±0.5% RH at 100 °C. In general, these sensors provide greater resolution at temperatures >90 °C than capacitive and resistive sensors, and can be used in applications where these sensors would not survive.

3.2.3 Capacitive humidity sensors

Capacitive humidity sensors consist of a substrate on which a thin film of polymer or metal oxide is deposited between two conductive electrodes. The sensing surface is coated with a porous metal electrode to protect it from contamination and exposure to condensation. The substrate is typically glass, ceramic, or silicon. The incremental change in the dielectric constant of a capacitive humidity sensor is nearly directly proportional to the relative humidity of the surrounding environment. The change in capacitance is typically 0.2–0.5 pF for a 1% RH change, while the bulk capacitance is between 100 and 500 pF at 50% RH at 25 °C. Capacitive sensors are characterized by low temperature coefficients, their ability to function at high temperatures (up to 200 °C), full recovery from condensation, and reasonable resistance to chemical vapors. The response time ranges from 30 s to 60 s for a 63% R.H. step change. The typical uncertainty of capacitive sensors is ±2% RH from 5% to 95% RH with a two-point calibration. Capacitive sensors are limited by the distance the sensing element can be located from the signal conditioning circuitry. This is due to the capacitive effect of the connecting cable with respect to the relatively small capacitance changes of the sensor.

3.3 Wearable humidity sensors

Resistive sensors are usable for remote locations and are cost effective. Capacitive sensors provide wide R.H. range and condensation tolerance. Thermal conductivity sensors perform well in corrosive environments and at high temperatures.

However, it should be taken into account that the final product has to be integrated into a fabric, has to be comfortable for the user and has to require a minimal circuitry for signal processing. Thus, thermal conductivity humidity sensors are not wearable and resistive sensors typically need a more complex circuitry (resistances >1 KΩ even for low relative humidity values require expensive and complex electronics) than capacitive sensors.

For these reasons we chose to study a wearable capacitive sensor although an attempt with a resistive-response hollow fibre was performed.

Bearing in mind the possibility of integrating the sensor in an industrial process, three different research lines were followed in parallel during the first year of activity:

a) Weaving conductive yarns coated with hydrophilic polymers.
b) Testing composite polymeric hollow fibres which vary their resistivity when water vapour is absorbed by the conducting polymer.
c) Using a layer of hydrophilic polymer as a dielectric between two plates made out of conductive fabrics.

The first and the third approaches are based on the same capacitive principle. The idea is to use conductive yarns or fabrics as the plates of a capacitor whose dielectric is hydrogel. Hydrogel is a jelly-like polymer, which is water-insoluble and so absorbent that it can contain over 99% water. The considerable water content gives a high degree of flexibility to the sensor making it suitable for integration into garments.

The capacitance is given by the well-known formula:

$$C = \varepsilon_o \varepsilon_r \frac{A}{D}$$

where C is the capacitance, $\varepsilon_0 = 8.854 \cdot 10^{-12}$ F/m is the permittivity of free space, ε_r is the relative static permittivity of the material between the plates, also called dielectric constant, A is the area of each plate, and d is the distance between the plates. In its normal state, hydrogel has a low dielectric constant but when it absorbs water vapor, this value increases enormously. This increase is generally much greater than the increase in the distance of the plates, thus the capacitance of the sensor increases as a result.

Two hydrogels were tested. Polyvinyl alcohol, PVA (Celvol 805, Celanese) and cellulose acetate butyrate, CAB. PVA and CAB have low dielectric constants, 2 and 5 respectively, compared to ~80 of water at 25 °C.

PVA hydrogel films were prepared by casting a 2 % w/w PVA solution in water in a Petri dish with the addition of polyacrylic acid (PAA) as a crosslinker.

Calibrating the increment of capacitance with the amount of water gives the relationship between capacitance and sweat rate.

3.3.1 Test system

A test system was prepared that allowed the flow of air at different degrees of humidity obtained by mixing dry air and saturated water vapor in different proportions. Air of chromatographic quality was supplied at a pressure of 3 bar by a zero air generator (Domnick Hunter, mod. UHP-35ZA) to a distributor from which several gas lines came out. For each line, a valve and a mass flow controller provided a flow of perfectly dry air in the range 0 e 500 ml/min. In the saturated water vapor line (Fig. 21) the dry air was bubbled into a glass vessel containing milliQ water at 50 °C and then cooled in a pipe coil at 25 °C. By mixing dry air and saturated water vapor in various proportions, all the possible relative humidity values (R.H. 0-100%) were obtained. To avoid artifacts due to the inertia of the system (the time needed to reach a stable set-up humidity value), a four-way valve was used either to convey the same flow of dry air or test vapor into the flow-through chamber housing the sensor. The relative humidity of the outcoming air was checked by a thermo-hygrometer, Delta Ohm Digital DO9406), while the sensor impedance was monitored by a precision LCR meter, Agilent E4980A, working at 1 kHz. These instruments were connected to a PC by a RS-232 and USB interface respectively.

An application written in Labview was developed to control the test system and to acquire data in a reproducible way.

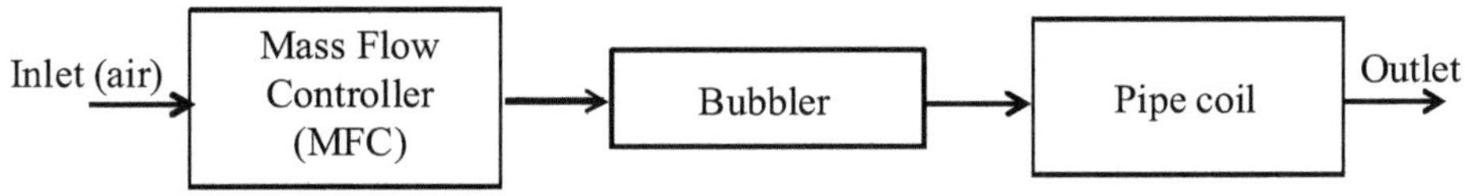

Fig. 21. Block diagram of the saturated water vapour line.

The software program has several important features among of which the most significant are:

1. It sets and saves up to 100 independent experimental set-up lines where each line includes the control of three mass-flow controllers (MFCs), the valve position, and duration of the measure and sample time.
2. It saves and recalls the set-ups.
3. Results are saved in an Excel file and/or a file for each set-up line.
4. Graphs of the values of the MFCs are immediately visible while typing to design personalised test curves.
5. The set-up lines can be shuffled or randomized.

3.4 Sensors based on conductive yarns coated with hydrophilic polymers

In this approach, the capacitive sensor is created by weaving two coated conductive yarns. This kind of sensor is very attractive and promising since it is suitable for integration in an industrial process by a textile company.

To choose the best yarn, two parameters are important:

- Electrical conductance
- Mechanical adhesion of the PVA-based hydrogel on the yarn (PVA is currently used in several industrial processes to protect textile fibres during mechanical handling. It is then easily washed away).

For this reason, several types of yarns, i.e. copper and stainless steel combined with natural or polymeric fibres such as linen and cotton, were tried out. Moreover, various percentages of material were considered. The types of yarns which have been tested are: a) 80% polyester / 20% Stainless steel fibres, b) 30% stainless steel fibres / 70% polyester, c) 51% cotton / 49% metallic stainless steel, d) multifilament yarn in 100% stainless steel, e) cotton / metallic copper and f) linen / metallic copper.

On the market there are no yarns coated with suitable hydrophilic polymers, hence a lab-scale set-up was prepared (Fig. 22).

A motor-controlled syringe pushes the polymer into a branch of a Teflon Y junction, while in the other branch a metallic fibre passes, pulled by a stepping motor.

After the output of the syringe, by a diameter selector disk, it is possible to remove the excess of polymer and set the desired diameter of the coated yarn, which is then dried by a constant flow of hot air. The yarn then reaches its final state and is recollected.

The software program that controls the system was written in Labview and also allows various sequential configurations to be set up to test the effects of different speeds on the quality of the resulting yarns.

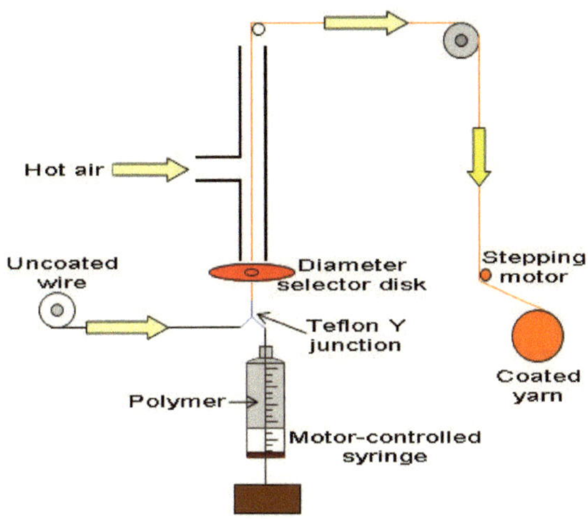

Fig. 11. Lab-scale set-up to coat yarns with a polymer.

Tables 5 and Fig. 23 show the results of preliminary tests on various wires coated with polyvinyl alcohol (PVA).

Table 5. Yarns tested in the preliminary coating experiments.

Wire/Yarn	Composition	Average thickness (mm)	Average PVA coating thickness (mm)
1	70% polyester / 30% stainless steel	0.045	0.2-0.4
2	80% polyester / 20% stainless steel	0.077	0.2-0.4
3	51% cotton / 49% stainless steel	0.050	0.2
4	Copper / Linen	0.121	0.2
5	Cotton / 2 wires of copper	0.162	0.2
6	Cotton / Ag^+	0.029	0.2

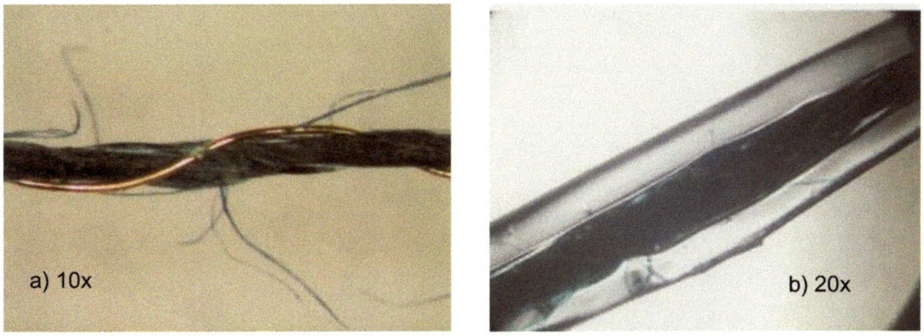

Fig. 12. Copper/linen wire before (a) and after (b) the coating.

The thickness of the coating mainly depends on the speed of the yarn through the solution and on the physical properties of the liquid, as calculated by Landau-Levich for Newtonian fluids:

$$h = 0.94\frac{(\eta v)^{2/3}}{\gamma_{LV}^{1/6}(\rho g)^{2/3}} \quad (1.7)$$

where h is the coating thickness, η is the viscosity of the solution, γ_{LV} is the liquid-vapour surface tension, ρ is the density of the solution, g is the acceleration of gravity, and v is the speed of the yarn. However, in order to achieve better reproducibility, several coating thicknesses were obtained by varying the diameter of the hole in the disk. Good results, with no uncoated regions as confirmed under the microscope, were achieved with an average thickness of 200 µm (Fig. 24).

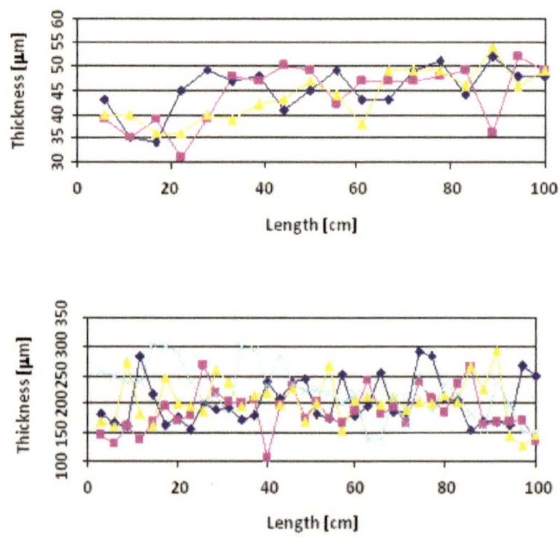

Fig. 13. Thickness of a stainless steel/polyester yarn: (top) uncoated, average thickness 40 µm and (bottom) coated, average thickness 200 µm samples.

A sensor patch was prepared by weaving coated and uncoated conductive yarns in a loom (Fig. 25).

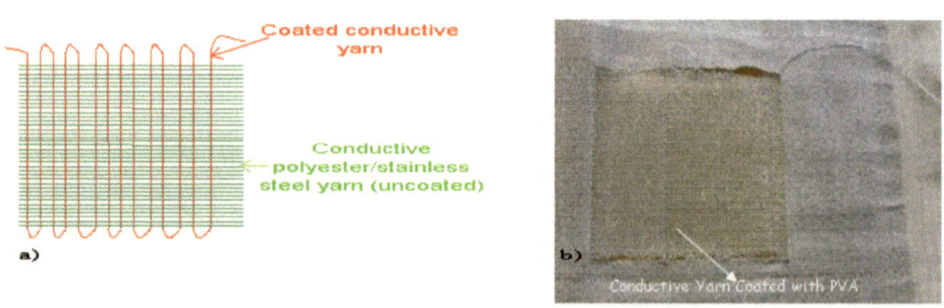

Fig. 14. Pattern a) and detail b) of the sensor patch.

Unfortunately, although the patch had great breathability, it revealed very low capacity values and extremely low signals when exposed to humidity, probably due to the low surface area of the capacitor plates. A different configuration was tried by spiraling the uncoated yarn around the coated one, but the resulting yarn was too fragile.

3.5 Sensors based on conductive polymer fibres

Santa Fe Science Technology supplied doped polypirrole and polyaniline composite conductive hollow fibres (Table 6), which vary their resistivity when the polymer absorbs water vapour. These fibres are industrially produced and can be integrated into garments.

Table 6. Resistance of several polypyrrole fibres.

Hollow Fibre	Dopant	Resistance (KΩ)	
Polypyrrole composite	Anthraquinone Sulphonate	Fibre 1	53
		Fibre 2	54.2
		Fibre 3	52.8
Polypyrrole composite	p-toluenesulphonate	Fibre 1	45.7
		Fibre 2	40.2
Polypyrrole composite	Naphtalene sulphonate	Fibre 1	704
Polyaniline	Phosphoric Acid	Fibre 1	n.m.

The housing chamber, used in the test system described in Section 3.3.1 is shown in Fig. 26.

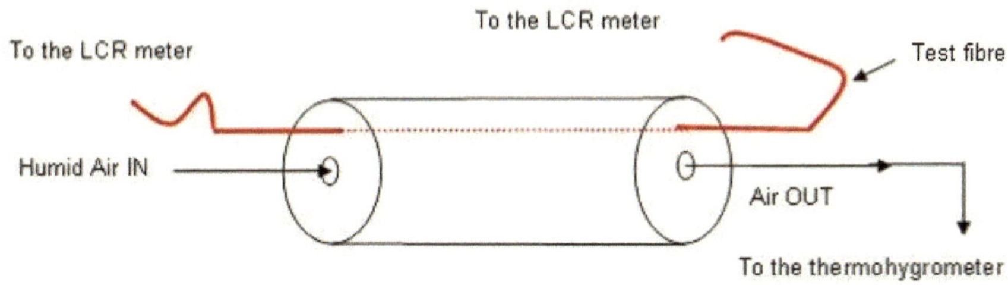

Fig. 15. The experimental set-up.

Three different samples of polypyrrole fibre doped with anthraquinone sulphonate (PPY/AS) were tested as humidity sensors, named fibres 1, 2 and 3 respectively. The test consisted of increasing the humidity values from 10% to 80 % (ascending series), followed by decreasing them to 10% (descending series). The resistance of fibre 1 as a function of time at various degrees of humidity is reported in Fig. 27 (fibres 2 and 3 show a similar behaviour).

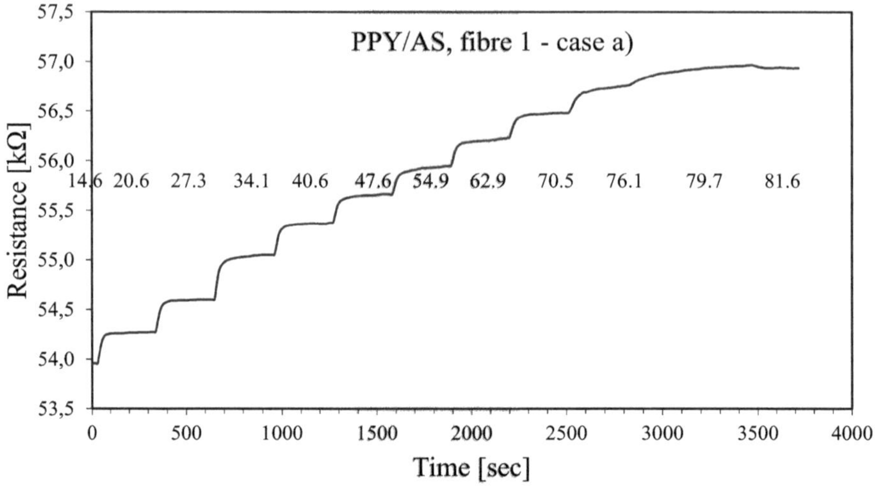

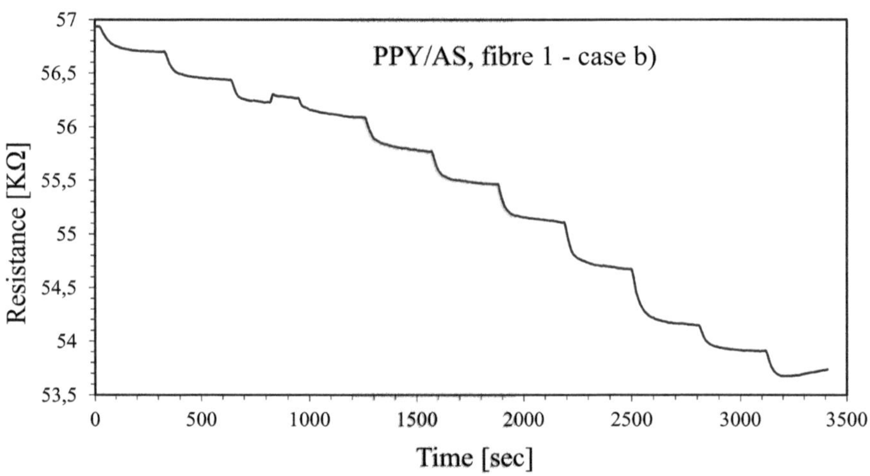

Fig. 16. Resistance of PPY/AS fibre 1 as a function of time at different degrees of humidity (reported in the graph): a) ascending series, b) descending series.

Fig. 28 shows a good linear behavior of the R.H.% - Resistance curve.

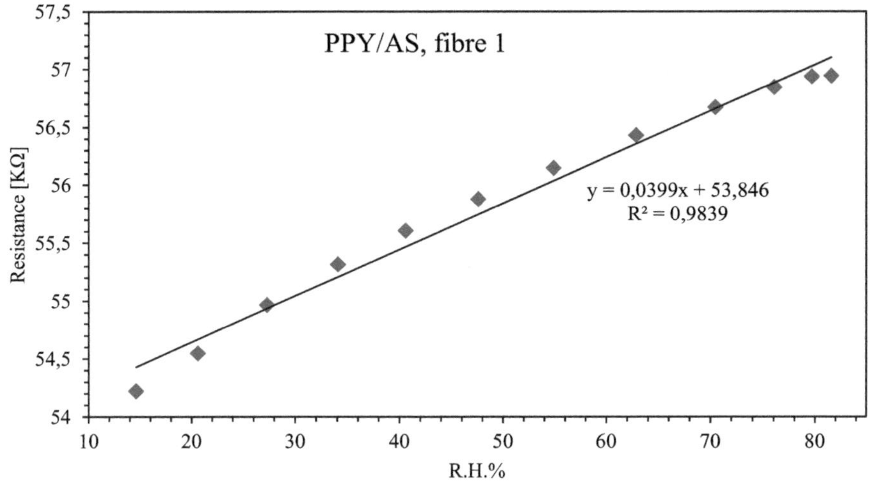

Fig. 17. Relationship between R.H. and resistance (average values) for fibre 1.

The PPY/AS fibre 1 and 2 responses to a variation of humidity of about 6% in two different regions are reported in Figs. 29 and 30.

The fibre shows quite a short response time in the low humidity region (about 1 minute), which increases in the high humidity region. As a comparison, the commercial humidity sensor PHILIPS H1 used as reference has a response time of 3 minutes.

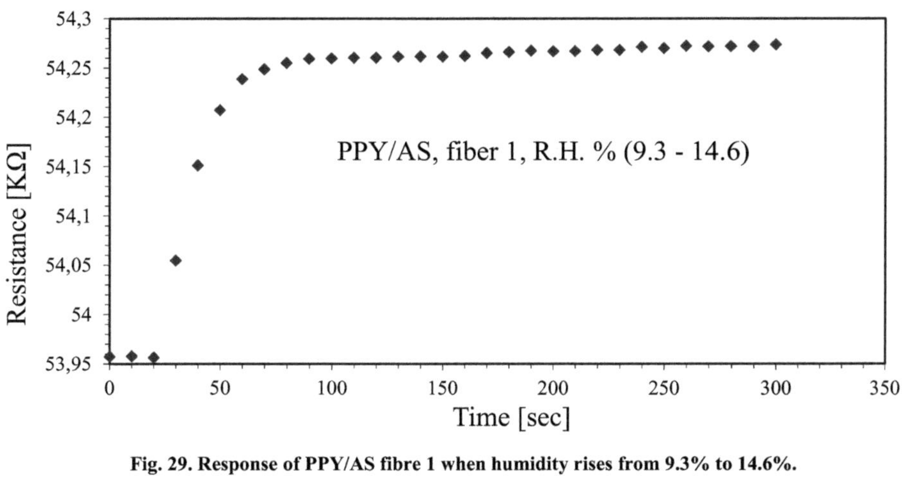

Fig. 29. Response of PPY/AS fibre 1 when humidity rises from 9.3% to 14.6%.

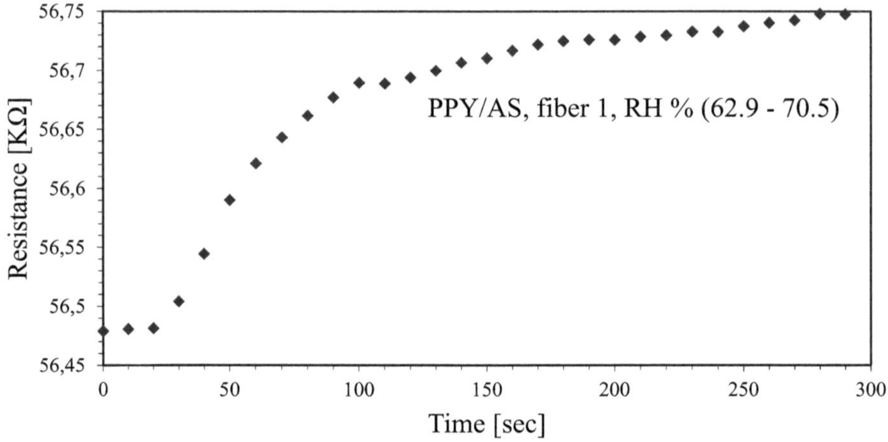

Fig. 18. Response of PPY/AS fibre 1 when humidity rises from 62.9% to 70.5%.

This trend to increase the response time and decrease the response amplitude to the same humidity variation is better seen in Fig. 31, which reports the normalized response of the fibre to the same variation in humidity in different regions. A similar behaviour was observed in PPY/AS fibre 2 and PPY/AS fibre 3.

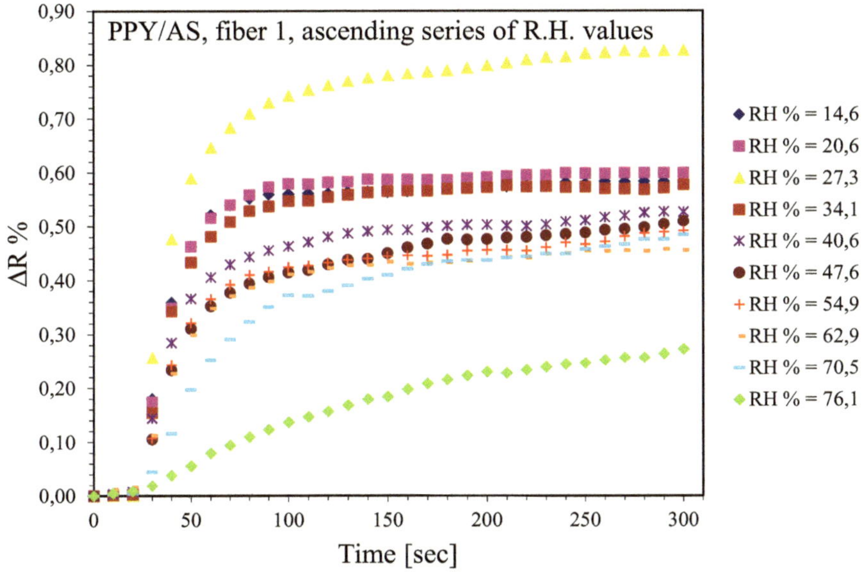

Fig. 19. Percentage variations of resistance of PPY/AS fibre 1 to a rising step of humidity of about 6% in different regions.

The calibration curves for the three tested fibres are reported in Fig. 32, where the data obtained in the ascending (A) a descending series (D) were plotted separately. All the fibres show a linear behaviour in the region 0–70 % R.H. A minimal hysteresis can be seen in fibre 1, while the best performance was obtained with fibre 2. There is good reproducibility among the three fibres.

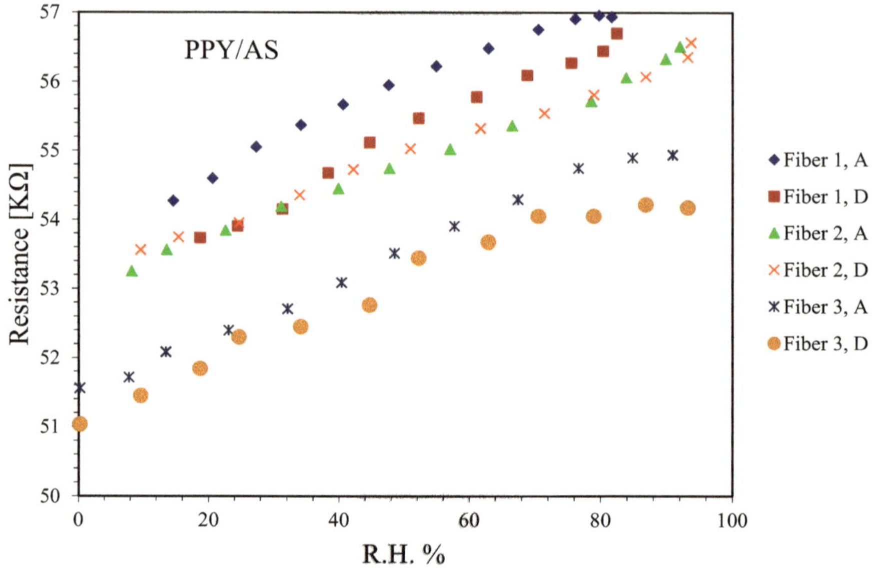

Fig. 20. Calibration curves for the three PPY/AS fibres, ascending (A) and descending (D) series.

A similar series of measurements was taken with the other polypyrrole fibres doped with p-toluenesulphonate (PPY/TS) and naphtalene sulphonate (PPY/NS), but the results were not so promising (Figs. 33 and 34). A notable difference was observed between the ascending and descending series, the latter characterized by much less noise.

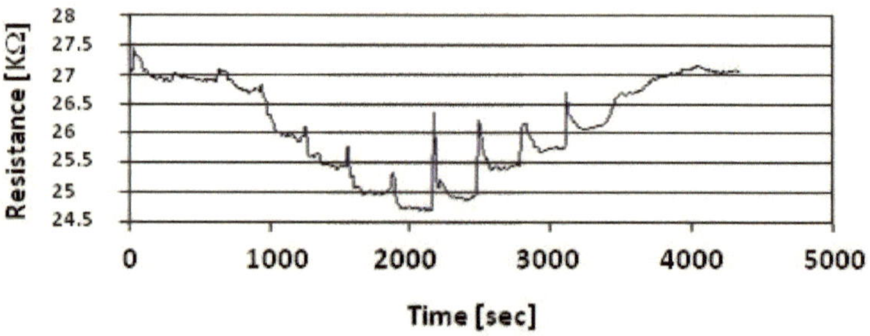

Fig. 21. Resistance of PPY/TS fibre 1 as a function of time at different degrees of R. H. (3%÷90%) function of time at different degrees of R. H. (3%÷90%).

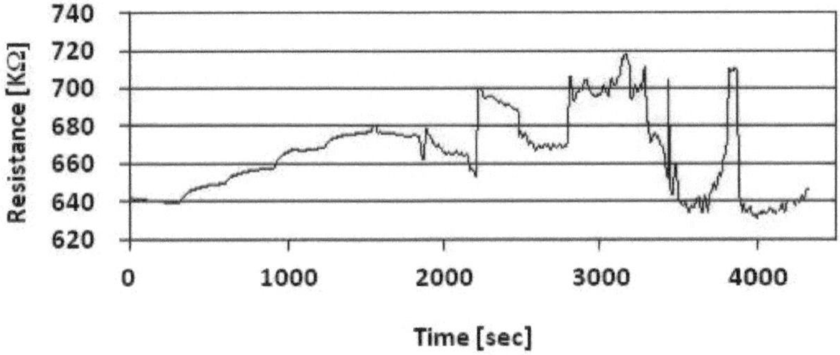

Fig. 22. of PPY/NS fibre 1 as a function of time at different degrees of R.H. (3%÷90%).

Polypyrrole fibres doped with anthraquinone sulphonate, 2-naphtalene sulphonate and p-toluene sulphonate respectively were tested by measuring resistance values with different degrees of humidity. The fibres doped with anthraquinone sulphonate showed a linear characteristic allowing it to be used as a humidity sensor in the range 0÷70%. The response time was short compared to other commercial devices (1 minute), although an increasing trend was observed with increasing humidity. The advantage of these fibres is their potential to be weaved into textiles, but the mechanical properties need to be improved to do this. A second batch of fibres was tested with improved mechanical performances, but in this case the sensing properties were much worse.

The SFST fibres were very promising but their major drawback was their fragility, which makes them very difficult to use as wearable sensors. Furthermore, it is impossible to bend them and cutting is extremely dangerous and difficult since a short circuit soon occurs. To cut them, the only solution is to freeze them in liquid nitrogen first. This means that the other type of sensors is preferable, at least for the moment.

3.6 Sensors based on a layer of hydrophilic polymer between conductive fabrics

Another approach to make a capacitive sensor that can be easily integrated into a patch is to sandwich a thin film of polymer between two conductive fabrics (Fig. 35).

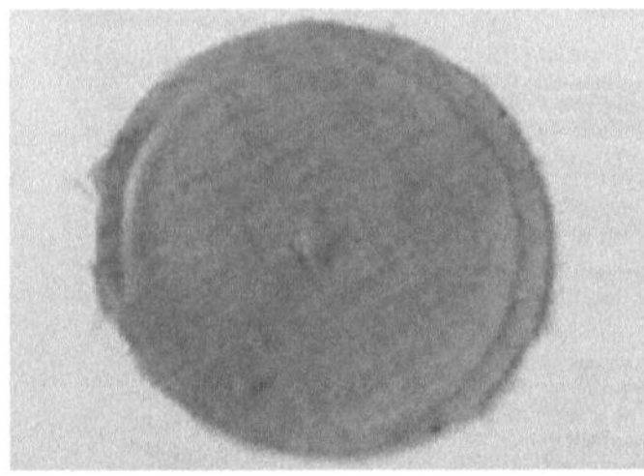

Fig. 23. Prototype of sensor made by PVA hydrogel between conductive fabrics.

The idea is to keep one of these sensors close to the skin, while the other, is separated by a semi-permeable membrane and placed further away from the skin, and is sensitive the external humidity. The global sensor works on a differential variation of the capacitance principle in order to evaluate the difference in humidity between the two sensors, thus allowing the sweat rate to be measured.

After a few attempts, the fabrics were coupled to the PVA hydrogel using a lab-scale thermo-press at a pressure of 400 atm and a temperature of 65 °C.

Fig. 36 shows the calibration curves for of a commercial humidity sensor (Philips H1) obtained in the lab in repeated measurements. The curves are very similar (except for a bias of about 15 pF which might be due to the electric connections) and this confirms that the test system functioned well. The calibration curves of the commercial and a prototype sensor are compared in Fig. 37.

The Philips H1 has an almost linear characteristic with a dynamic range of about 30 pF, while the prototype had a dynamic range of about 3.5 nF (more than one order of magnitude higher) but most of the variation was observed when the relative humidity exceeded 60%.

This result is very good in terms of placing the sensor between the membrane and the skin (where high humidity values are expected), but it needs improving in the low humidity region in order to place the sensor on the top of the membrane.

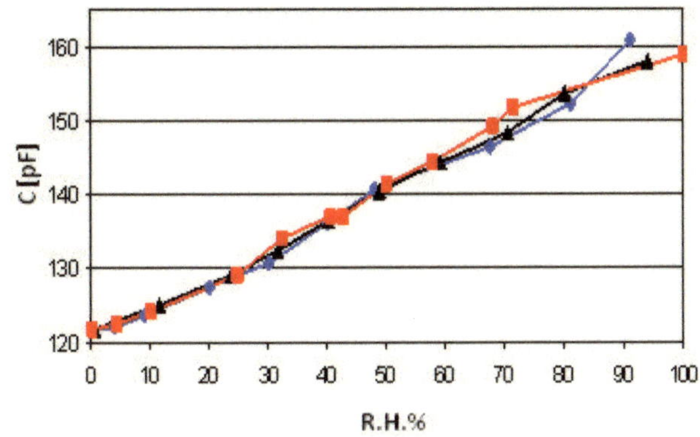

Fig. 24. Calibration curves of a commercial humidity sensor (Philips H1) left) from the data sheet and right) with repeated measurements using the calibration set-up.

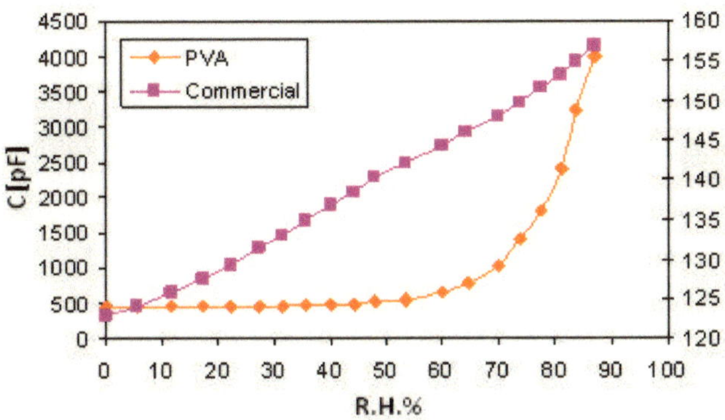

Fig. 25. Comparison of the capacitance of a coupled conductive fabrics/PVA sensor with a commercial humidity sensor (Philips H1).

Similar tests were carried out for a sensor prepared by gluing the conductive fabrics to a hydrophilic polyurethane layer supplied by Sofileta (Fig. 38). The glue was applied on the fabric in a controlled quantity and pre-polymerized at 100 °C, then coupled with PVA and pressed at 100°C. The polymerization of the glue was at 170 °C. The glue was selected based on its level of breathability. A remarkable capacitance variation (about 2 nF) was observed similar to the PVA sensor, but in this case the signal seemed far noisier.

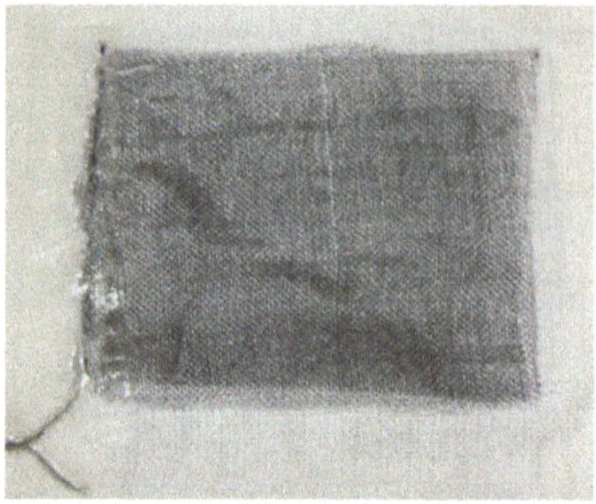

Fig. 38. Sweat rate sensor with a hydrophilic polyurethane layer.

Better results were achieved with a different configuration based on two humidity sensors separated by a fabric membrane. The sensing element was a thin cellulose acetate butyrate (CAB) film (thickness 21µm), purchased from Goodfellow, and with vacuum evaporated gold electrodes (thickness in the range of 2÷40 nm). CAB is an ester of cellulose with a permittivity of 5 at 1 KHz. Two thin cables were glued onto the electrodes with a conducting epoxy resin (8331-14 G, Mouser) for the electrical contacts (Fig. 39).

Fig. 39. Capacitive CAB sensor.

To assemble the sweat rate sensor, two pockets were created on the opposite sides of a textile semi-permeable membrane or a fabric net, by attaching a seamless net fabric (88% polyamide, 12% elasthane) to it with an ultrasonic welder. These pockets were used to house the humidity sensors close to the membrane/fabric net (Fig. 40). An 8x4 mm gasket was also glued to the intermediate layer to keep the sensor at the correct distance from the skin.

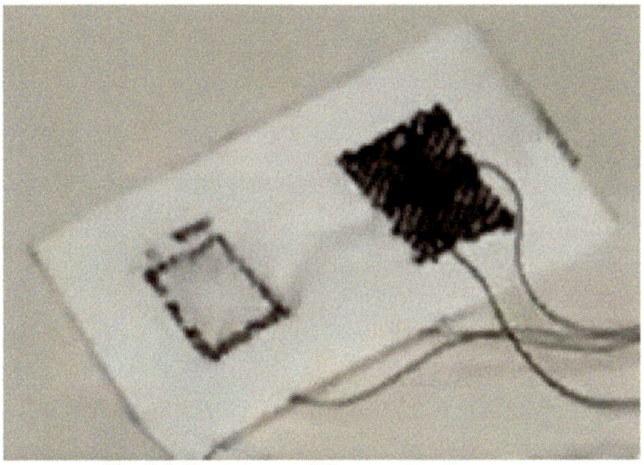

Fig. 26. Prototype of the sweat rate sensor.

The difference between the membrane and the fabric net depends on their different breathing capacity, which leads to different gradients. In fact, with the membrane separating the two humidity sensors, a higher humidity gradient is expected compared to the fabric net, which has a higher breathing capacity.

3.7 Test of the sweat rate sensor

One of the main problems of testing the sweat rate sensor was the definition of the test procedures. The main difficulty involved preparing a standard surface that would simulate the skin and be capable of delivering a controlled flow of water vapor at a stable rate. Furthermore, the membrane of the sweat rate sensor represented a barrier that would alter the equilibrium (in a similar way that a dress does on the skin) thus making the situation even more complex.
To choose the appropriate membrane/fabric net, a feasible procedure was defined by calculating the flow of water vapor through the membrane/fabric net by means of a mass balance after measuring the weight loss of a saturated salt solution, used as an emitting surface, in a defined duration of time (Fig. 41). Such solutions for obtaining stable and reproducible humidity values have been widely used to calibrate humidity sensors. The bottom part of a flow-through chamber was filled with one such solution, while the sweat rate sensor was used to separate the bottom and top parts of the chamber. In the top part, different humidity gradients were achieved by pumping air at a controlled degree of humidity. The flow of humidity through the sensor was evaluated by measuring the weight loss of the solution in a fixed length of time.

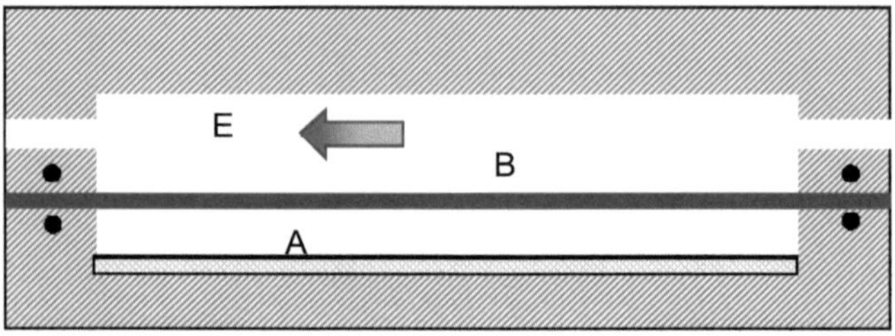

Fig. 27. Diagram of the test chamber used in the test procedures.

A chamber was designed and set up to test the idea (Fig. 42).

Fig. 28. Test chamber for the humidity and sweat rate sensor.

In the chamber, the saturated salt solution, which maintains a fixed humidity value, is contained in the bottom part and the whole chamber is placed on the scale. The upper part of the chamber can be flushed by a flow of air at a controlled humidity obtained by mixing dry air flows and saturated water vapor flows in different proportions. The flow values are regulated by two MFCs controlled by a PC running a software application written in Labview. Dry air is supplied by a zero air generator, while the saturated water vapor is obtained by bubbling air into distilled water at 50 °C and cooling the resulting vapor to 25 °C in a pipe coil. The chamber leans on the plate of a scale with a serial interface. A simple software application was developed to continuously monitor the chamber weight. Different humidity values can be generated by changing the solution, as shown in Table 7.

Table 7. Humidity values generated by different salt solutions [Handbook of Chemistry and Physics].

Salt (saturated in water)		R.H.(%) @25°C	@20°C
Lithium Chloride	LiCl	11.3 (±0.3)	12
Magnesium Chloride	MgCl	32.8 (±0.3)	33.1 (± 0.2)
Magnesium Nitrate	$Mg(NO_2)$	53.0 (±0.1)	55
Sodium Chloride	NaCl	75.3 (±0.1)	75.1 (± 0.1)
Potassium Chloride	K_2SO_4	97.3 (±0.5)	97.6 (± 0.5)

Table 8 shows the different kinds of membranes that were tested.

Table 8. Semi-permeable membranes used in the tests.

Membrane	Abbreviation	Composition	Thickness (μm)
Skintech N25	PU N25	Polyurethane	20
Skintech S400	SK 400	Polyurethane	25

The normalized weight loss observed with the different membranes when a saturated potassium chloride solution was used is reported in Fig. 43.

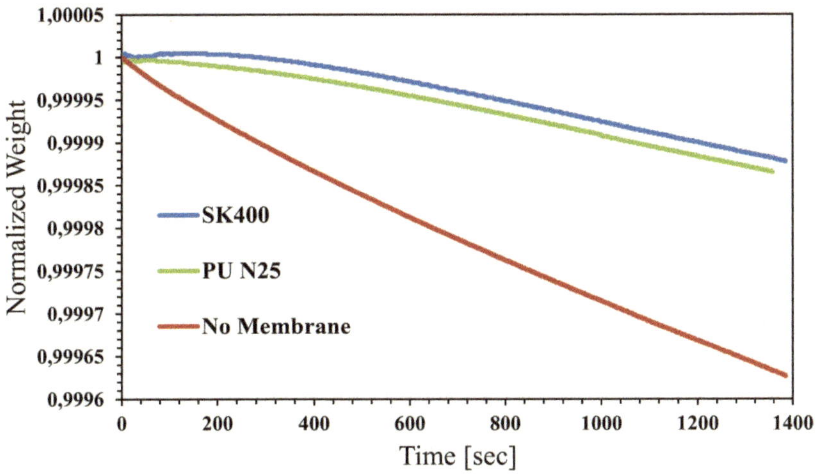

Fig. 29. Weight loss of the KCl saturated solution through the membranes.

The water flow across the membrane can be easily derived from the slope, once the surface area is known. However, the use of a membrane was found to have important drawbacks. In fact, the lifetime of the humidity sensor closer to the skin was dramatically shortened. Furthermore this calibration method is impractical in an industrial process.

A fabric net was thus preferable to separate the two humidity sensors, as it breathes better than the textile membranes. The permeability to vapour of a cotton lint and the two fabric net provided by Smartex were compared to the Skin-Tech membranes (Fig. 44).

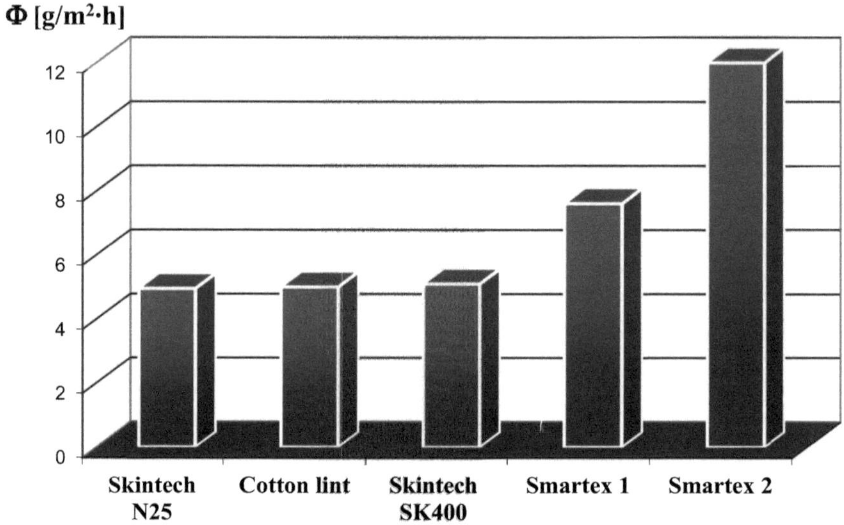

Fig. 30. Permeability of different membranes.

As was expected, the fabric nets showed a better permeability and were adopted to lengthen the lifetime of the humidity sensors and for the calibration system test, which is discussed in the following chapter.

References

[1] R. D. Mosteller, "*Simplified calculation of body-surface area*," New England Journal of Medicine, 317(17), pp. 1098, 1987.

[2] D. DuBois, and E. F. DuBois, "*A formula to estimate the approximate surface area if height and weight be known*," Archives of Internal Medicine, 17, pp. 863-871, 1916.

[3] G. E. Nilsson, "*Measurement of water exchange through skin*," Medical & Biological Engineering & Computing, 15, pp. 209-218, 1977.

[4] D. K. Roveti, "Choosing a Humidity Sensor: A Review of Three Technologies," www.sensorsmag.com, July, 2001.

Chapter 4 - Calibration of the sensors and results

4.1 Choice of body area for sweat sampling

The testing and calibration of sensors first entails defining the area of the body where the measurements will be performed.

Sweat samples, stimulated either by pilocarpine delivery via iontophoresis or by physical activity, were collected using filter paper from two healthy volunteers, a male and a female, on different body regions - calf, forearm and lower back - to estimate possible differences in sweat composition. Pilocarpine delivery is known to be the most practical method to induce sweating, but a sort of temporary adaptation was observed resulting in a decreased amount of collected sweat. However, for the limited set of available data, the stimulation technique did not seem to affect sweat composition.

Sodium and chloride concentrations in sweat are reported in Fig. 45 and 46, following the same pattern; starting from the left:

- Bars 1-2 represent a pooled average (all sweat concentration values, without any distinction between stimulation techniques and regions of collection) for the two volunteers;
- Bars 3-4 and 5-6 represent the averages of samples collected by pilocarpine and physical activity respectively (no distinction between regions of collection) for the two volunteers;

Bars 7-9 and 10-12 represent the averages of samples collected in different body regions (no distinction between samples collected by pilocarpine and physical activity) for the two volunteers, respectively.

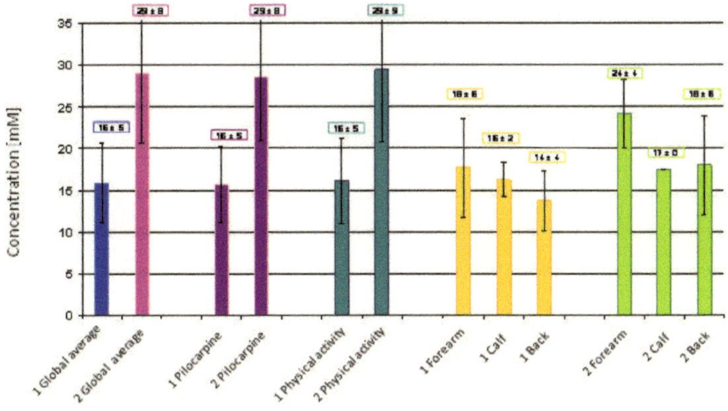

Fig. 31. Sodium concentrations in sweat: 1 = male, 2 = female

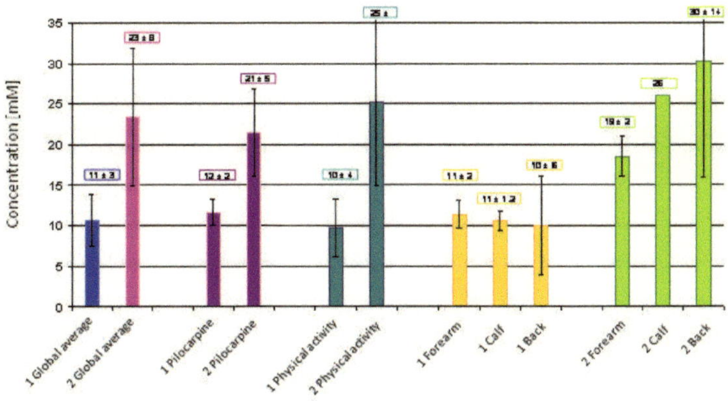

Fig. 46. Chloride concentrations in sweat: 1 = male, 2 = female.

Sodium and chloride are the most representative ions due to their concentrations and a difference is evident between male and female. Data concerning the concentrations of ammonium, calcium, potassium and magnesium are reported in Table 9.

Table 9. Sweat concentrations of Ammonium, Potassium, Magnesium and Calcium (mM).

Concentration [mM]	*Ammonium*		*Potassium*		*Magnesium*		*Calcium*	
	average	sd	average	sd	average	sd	average	sd
Global average (Male)	7	3	6	2	0.01	0.02	0.3	0.2
Global average (Female)	7	4	9	3	0.1	0.1	0.5	0.4
Pilocarpine (Male)	7	4	6	1	0.0	0.0	0.2	0.1
Pilocarpine (Female)	7	6	9	1	0.01	0.01	0.4	0.3
Physical activity (Male)	7	2	7	2	0.01	0.02	0.36	0.22
Physical activity (Female)	6	1	10	3	0.1	0.1	0.6	0.4
Forearm (Male)	7	1	7	2	0.01	0.01	0.3	0.2
Calf (Male)	4	2	6	0.5	0.01	0.02	0.2	0.1
Back (Male)	10	1	6	0	0.00	0.02	0.3	0.1
Forearm (Female)	9	1	10	3	0.1	0.1	0.7	0.3
Calf (Female)	1	0	8		0.0		0.1	
Back (Female)	3	1	8	2	0.1	0.09	0.5	0.3

No significant differences were observed in samples collected from different body regions. This result is not in contrast with those reported by [1] if the large inter-individual variability is taken into account.

The main conclusion is that it makes no difference in which of these body regions the conductivity sensor is placed. It is possible to locate the sensor patch in any of these body regions and to transfer conclusions regarding sweat stimulated by pilocarpine delivery to sweat stimulated by physical activity.

During testing it was observed that sweat production can vary between different people, and even in the same person there may be different behaviors on different days, as shown in Fig. 47.

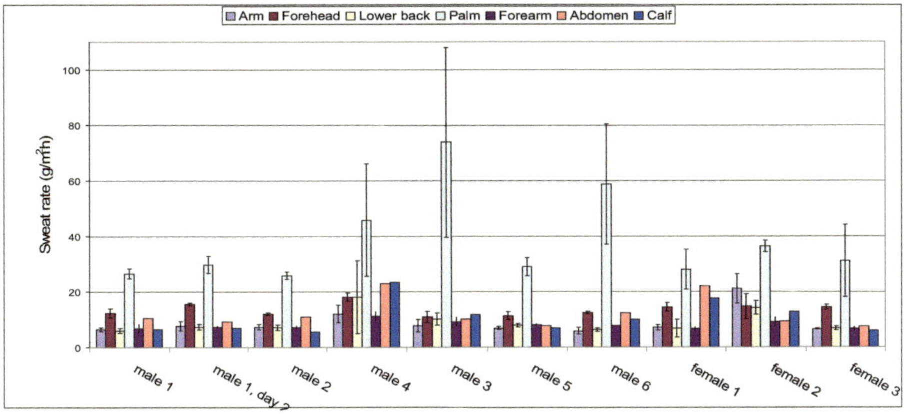

Fig. 32. Sweat rates measured in 9 volunteers at rest from different body regions: arm, forehead, lower back, palm, forearm, abdomen and calf.

Differences amongst individuals who are at rest are relatively small, and there are no significant differences in sweat rates in the various regions of the body. However, larger variations between these regions are observed during intense sweating after physical exercise (Fig. 48).

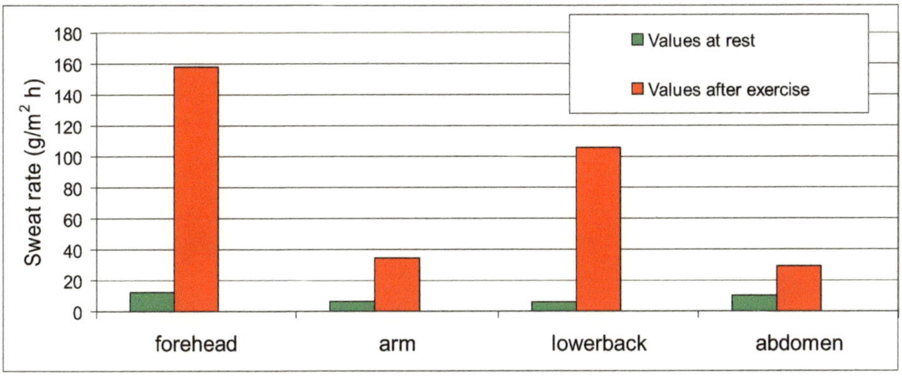

Fig. 48. Sweat rate values measured from different body regions in 6 volunteers during the trials.

Figs. 47 and 48 show that there are areas of the body where sweat production is more intensive, such as the forehead and arm. However, sweat production in the lower back is not particularly different from the majority of the other body areas; it has a wide surface and allows an easy placement of the sensor.

On the basis of these considerations, the lower back was selected as the location for the sensor patches, since it is one of the regions with the most intense sweating and large area to place the sensor.

4.2 Calibration of the sensors

The conductivity sensor was first calibrated by dipping it in solutions of 20, 40, 60 and 80 mM of Na+, which were verified by the Sweat Check analyzer 3100, Wescor. It was found that the sensor responded instantaneously and the results were stable and reproducible, as shown in Fig. 49.

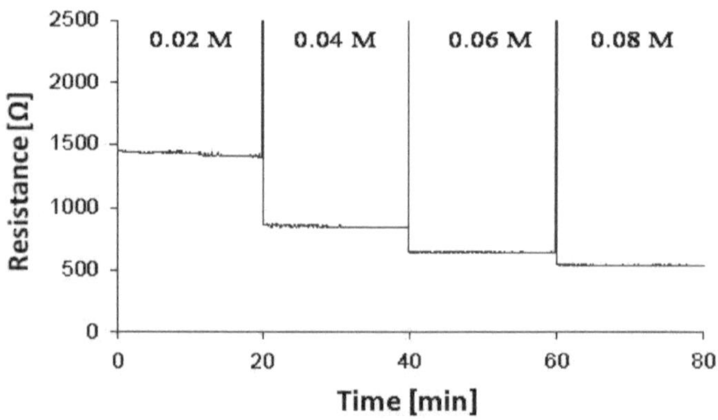

Fig. 33. Calibration of conductivity sensor in solution.

The sensor was then calibrated by gluing the patch onto the pump. The resulting equation was: $R \cdot k = 7.222$, where $R^2 = 0.9994$ and RMSE=0.036, (Fig. 50).

The amount of solution needed to wet the pump is not negligible; thus, the value of conductivity is strictly related to the sweat rate, which needs to be high enough to wet the pump.

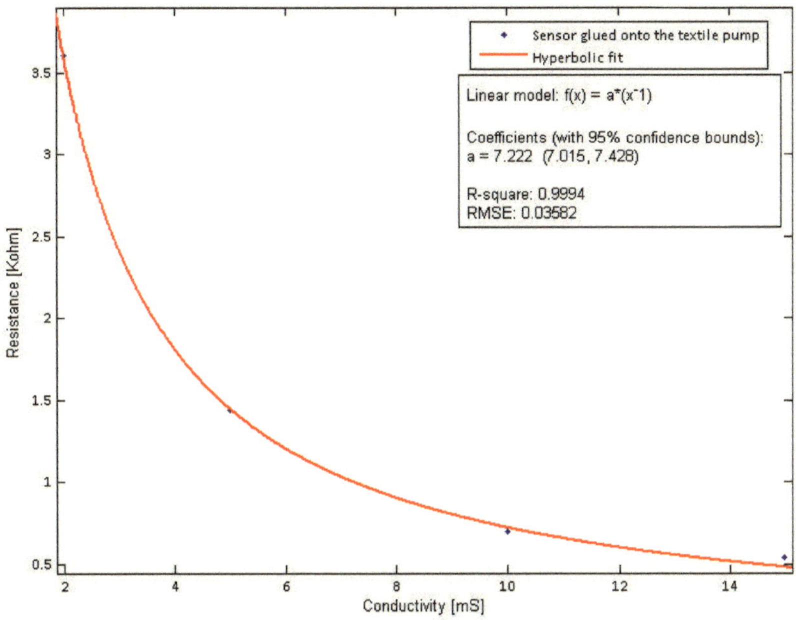

Fig. 34. Calibration of the conductivity sensor glued to the fabric pump.

Figs. 51 and 52 report the results of the first on-body test when the volunteer starts sweating, with the patch coupled to the fabric pump. The signal shows some noise but the values are in the physiological range.

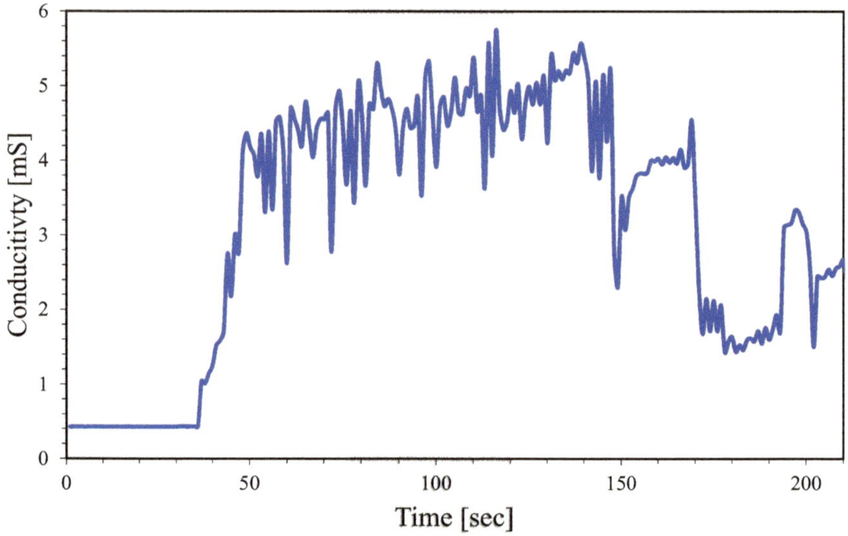

Fig. 35. Sweat conductivity of the volunteer during the on-body test

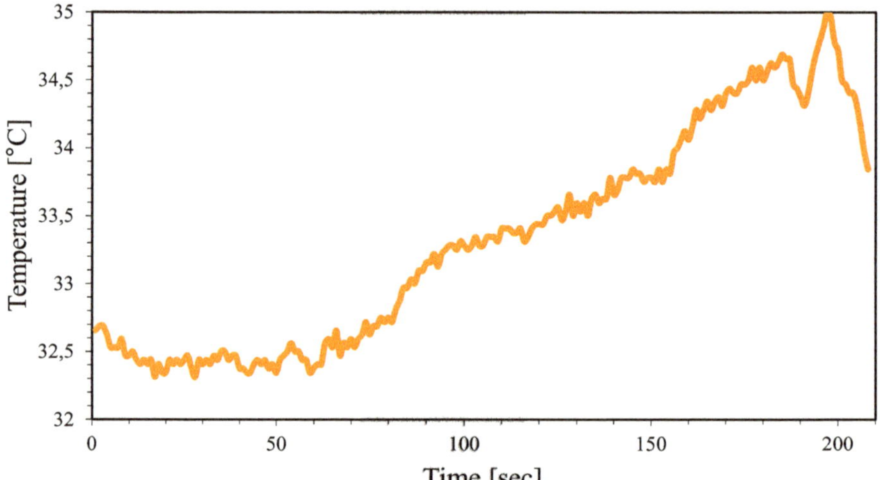

Fig. 52. Sweat temperature of the volunteer during the on-body test.

As mentioned in Section 3.7, it was decided to remove the membrane in order to obtain conditions close to those of practical use; therefore, calibrations with an open chamber were performed.

With the configuration of the open chamber, the humidity value on the top side of the sensor was fixed to the lab humidity value, and the only way to obtain different gradients was to change the saturated salt solutions inside the chamber.

A sufficiently stable emitting surface may be obtained by soaking a sponge with de-ionized water or a saturated salt solution. In this case, flow values can vary by heating the sponge at different temperatures. Unfortunately, this approach proved lengthy and unsuitable for obtaining reproducible results.

Excellent results were obtained with a slightly different approach.

A constant water flow was obtained by placing a sponge into a 1.2 cm high Petri dish, soaking it with de-ionized water and controlling the temperature. The two humidity sensors were placed at a distance of 1 cm in height. The flow rate was calculated from the weight loss over time in the Petri dish as measured using a laboratory scale (Adventurer Pro, OHAUS) connected to a PC via a RS-232 interface and acquired by a program written in Labview. Different flow rates can be obtained by heating the chamber at different temperatures.

Sensor capacitances were acquired by designing a scanning system that can return the two values simultaneously. An LCR meter (Agilent E4980A) was coupled to a switch (Agilent 3499A) by a multiplexer module (Agilent N2266A). To link the instruments, a GPIB connection was used, while to connect the devices under test (DUT) i.e. the capacitive sensors, an external board was made.

The BNC cable configuration used was the four-terminal pair (4TP), which guarantees the highest accuracy over wide impedance and frequency ranges.

However, a discrepancy in measurement values among channels may occur. The measurement error increases due to the residual impedance and the stray admittance in the scanning system.

To compensate for these errors, the channels used for the capacitive measurements were calibrated by a reference capacitor.

The scanning system was fully controlled by a new feature of the software mentioned in Chapter 3, written in Labview, which was also able to set the desired relative humidity by controlling three mass flow meters and to monitor in real time the temperature and relative humidity provided by the thermo-hygrometer D0-9406. The software can acquire signals from eight channels and allows the variable (C, R, L, Z or Y) to be set which has to be measured for each channel independently (Fig. 53).

Furthermore, an important feature, not visible in the screenshot, is the possibility of having the graph of the humidity gradient in real time. The parameters of calibration may be set in dedicated fields and the software shows the results in a chart.

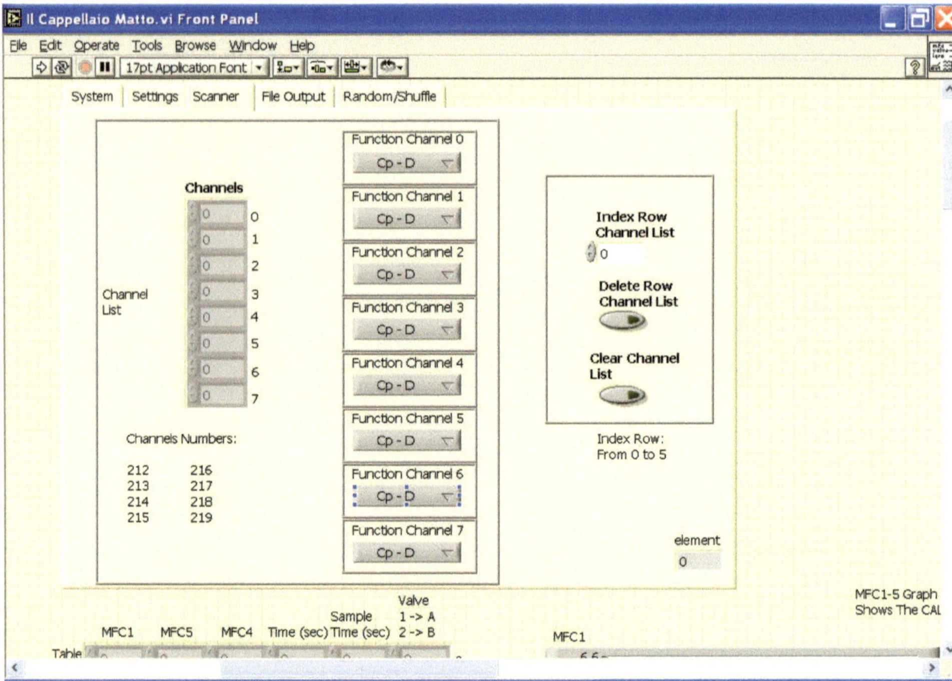

Fig. 36. A detail of a screenshot of the software written in Labview to control the testing system.

Table 10 shows the results of the calibration after five repeated tests.

Table 10. Results of the calibration after five repeated tests

Temperature [°C] **(mean values)**	Φ [g/m²·h] **(mean values)**	ΔC [pF] **(mean values)**
26	150	1.3
31	375	7
36	660	8.5
46	1120	11.5
60	2000	18

A linear characteristic is observed for flow and capacitance gradients at different temperatures (Figs. 54 and 55).

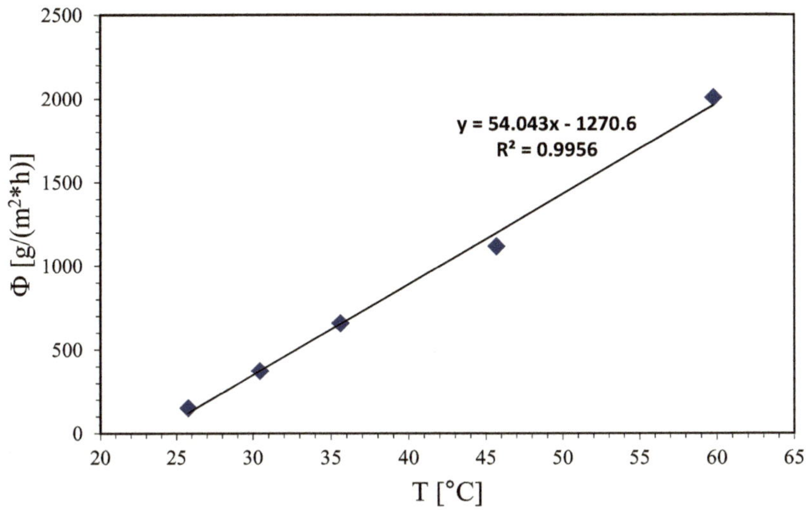

Fig. 37. Flow - Temperature characteristic.

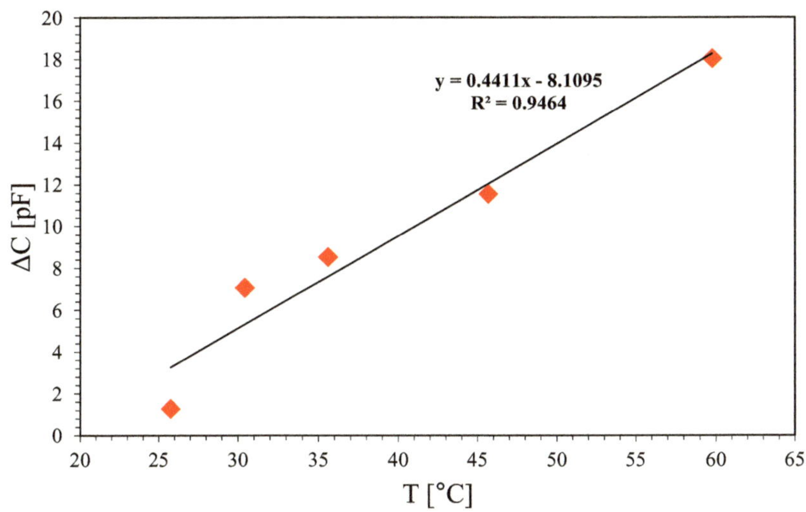

Fig. 38. Capacitance gradient – Temperature characteristics.

The calibration line of the sweat rate sensor is reported in Fig. 56. A good linear approximation of the dependence of flow from the capacitance (i.e. humidity) gradient was obtained.

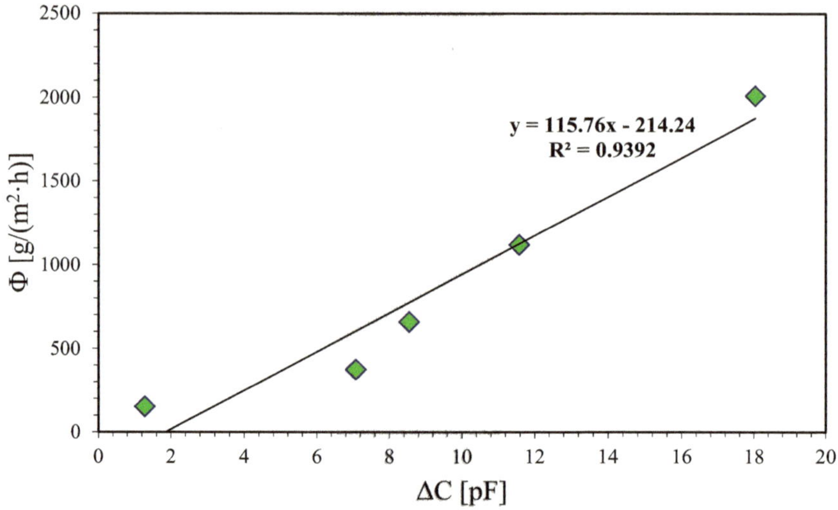

Fig. 39. Calibration of the sweat rate sensor.

The resulting calibration equation, $\Phi=115.76 \bullet \Delta C-214.24$, was then tested in on-body tests.

4.3 Results

CSEM has specifically designed a device to retrieve data from all of the developed sensors. The system is shown in Fig. 57 where it is possible to see the external interface connecting the pH and the multi-patch (sodium, temperature and conductivity sensors).

Data are transmitted by Bluetooth® to a PC in a binary format, which is preferable due to its low power consumption. The graph is shown in Tinyviewer (by CSEM) which is the visualization utility included with the BIOTEX unit. The conversion in a decimal format was done using Matlab.

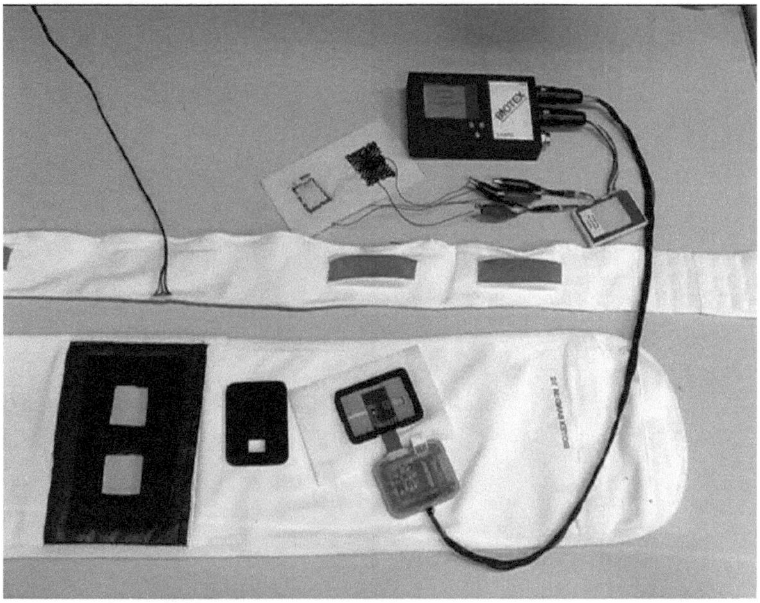

Fig. 40. Full view of waistbands and electronics.

Before starting the tests, all measurements were taken using LCR Agilent E4980A. Several calibrations were therefore performed with both the LCR and the BIOTEX Control Unit to compare their performances. A slight bias of about 8-10 pF was observed between the two units.

The sensors were integrated and tested on healthy volunteers to ensure that the sensors were functioning correctly.

The integration of a complex system poses several issues such as interference between different signals, data management etc. that need to be solved before involving people with health problems.

In exercise trial 1, the volunteer was a male who cycled for about half an hour.

The temperature (Fig. 58) continuously increased during the trial suggesting that the subject was not sweating much. The same conclusion was obtained from the data relevant to conductivity (Fig. 59).

The amount of sweat produced was insufficient to wet the pump and obtain a useful signal from the sweat conductivity sensor.

Sweat rate data could not be gathered during this trial due to a problem with the connections.

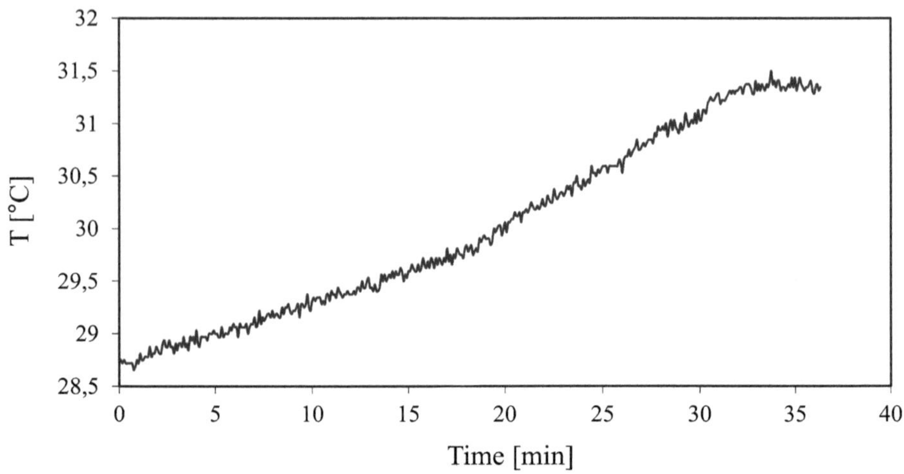

Fig. 58. Temperature data during exercise trial 1.

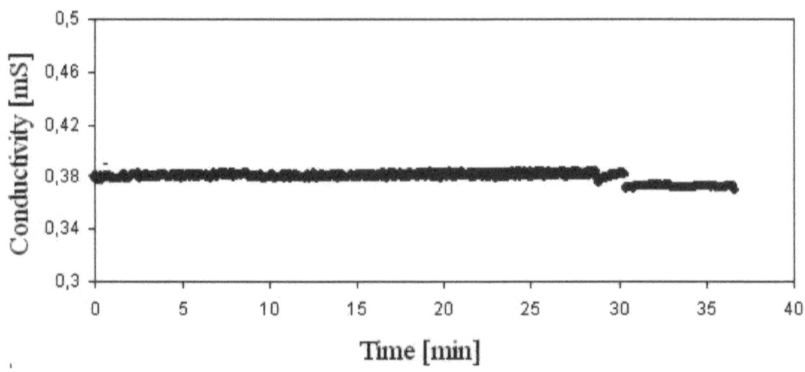

Fig. 59. Conductivity data during exercise trial 1.

In exercise trial 2, the sweat rate sensor located on the lower back was connected to the BIOTEX Unit, while another sweat rate sensor was placed on the forearm and measured using the commercial LCR. The male volunteer cycled for about 30 minutes.

The results showed that data acquired by the BIOTEX Unit is very noisy, especially on one of the two channels. In addition, data obtained from one of the two humidity sensors that are part of the sweat rate sensor were of very little value. The raw data acquired from the other sensor by the LCR meter showed almost no spikes (Figs. 60 and 61).

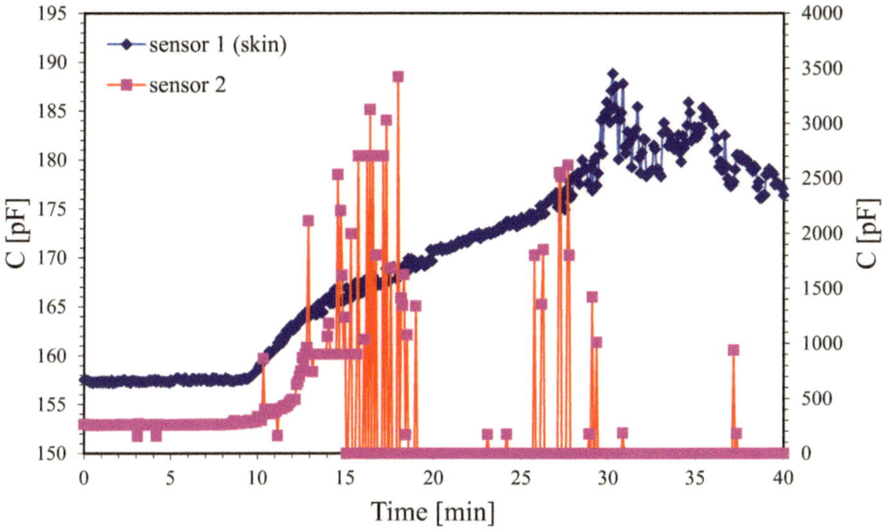

Fig. 60. Capacitance values of the two humidity sensors that make up the sweat rate sensor located on the lower back measured by the BIOTEX Unit during exercise trial 2 (Sensor 1 is the one close to the skin).

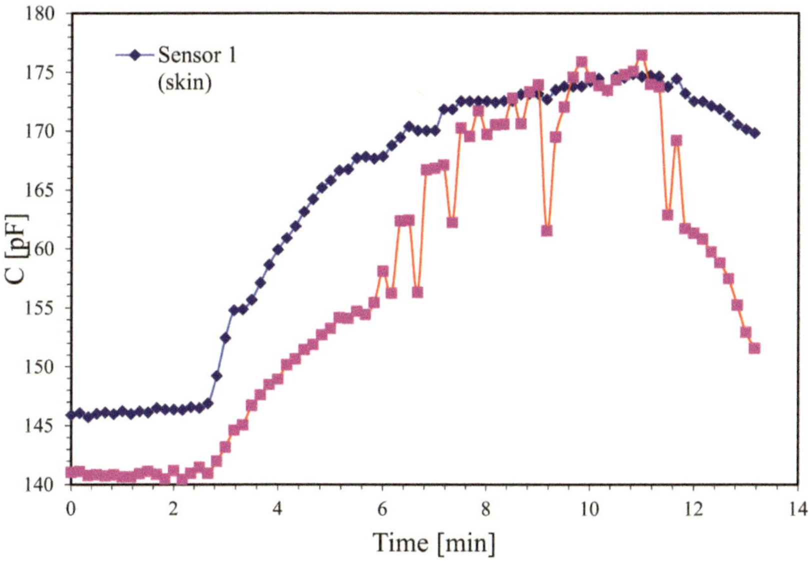

Fig. 41. Capacitance values of the two humidity sensors that make up the sweat rate sensor located on the forearm measured by the LCR meter during exercise trial 2 (Sensor 1 is the one close to the skin).

Sweating was insufficient to produce a signal from the sweat conductivity sensor glued to the fabric pump (Fig. 62). Poor contact between the multi-parametric patch and fabric pump was suspected.

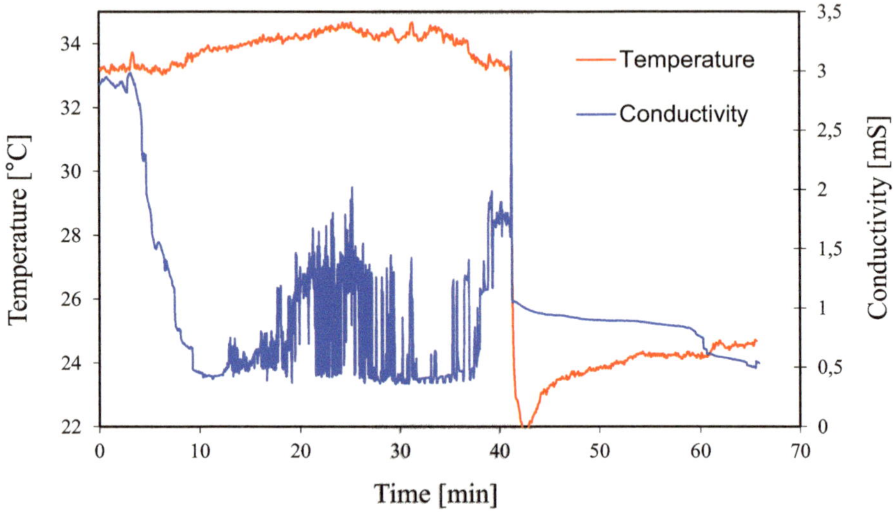

Fig. 42. Temperature and conductivity data during exercise trial 2.

In exercise trial 3, the volunteer cycled for one hour before stopping. The sweat rate sensor, connected to LCR, resulted in a much smaller but measurable gradient with no spikes (Figs. 63, 64 and 65).

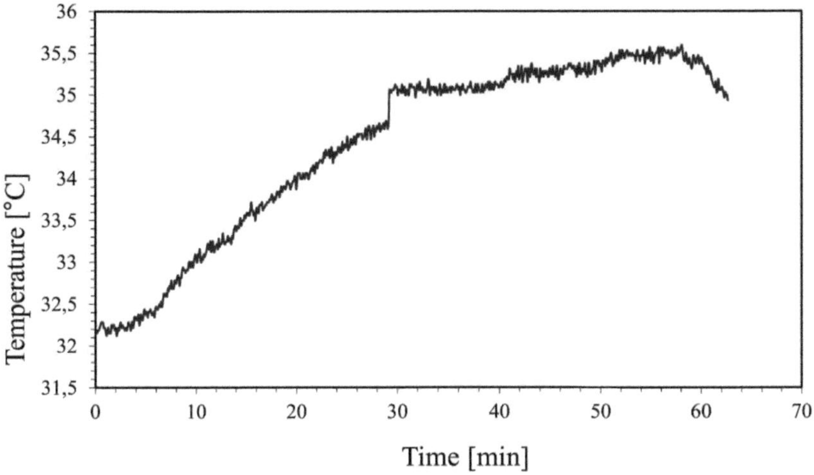

Fig. 63. Temperature data during exercise trial 3.

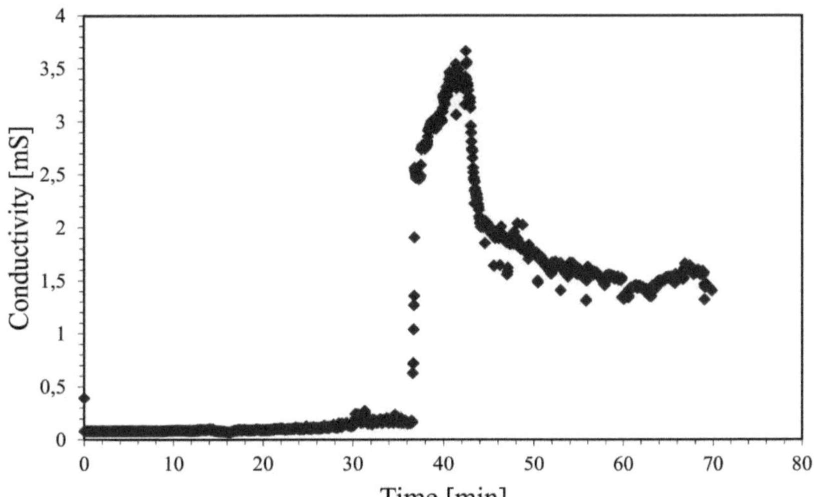

Fig. 43. Conductivity data during exercise trial 3.

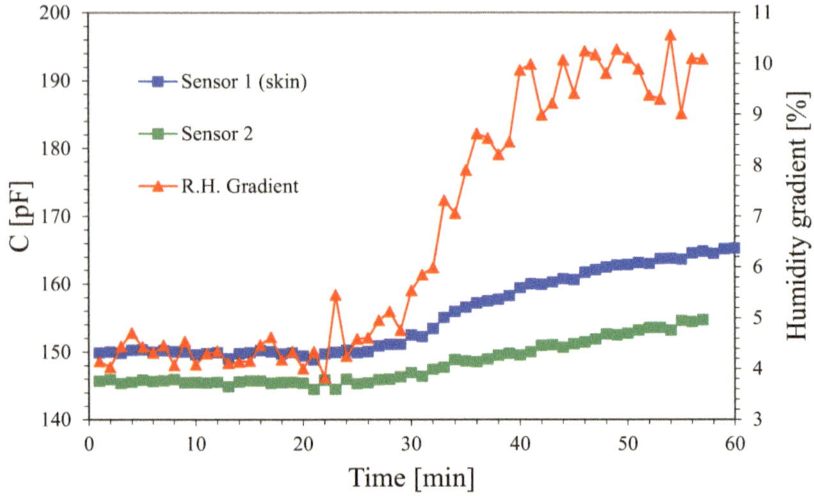

Fig. 44. Capacitances acquired by the LCR meter and humidity gradient obtained during exercise trial 3.

In exercise trial 4, the volunteer was a female who cycled for 25 minutes. On the basis of previous experiences, to improve the conductivity signal, a layer of neoprene was inserted under the lid of the fabric pump in order to exert pressure on the multi-parametric patch and keep it in closer contact with the fabric pump. Furthermore, the patch was placed vertically to allow the fabric pump to collect more sweat (Figs. 66 and 67).

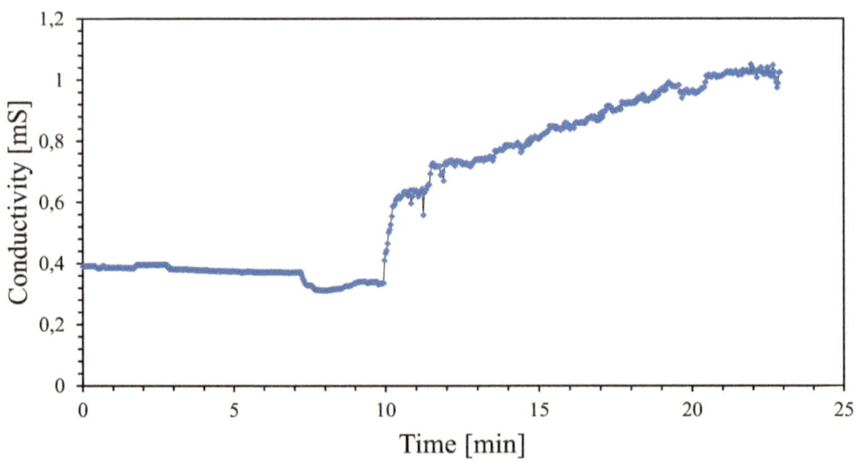

Fig. 45. Conductivity data during trial 4.

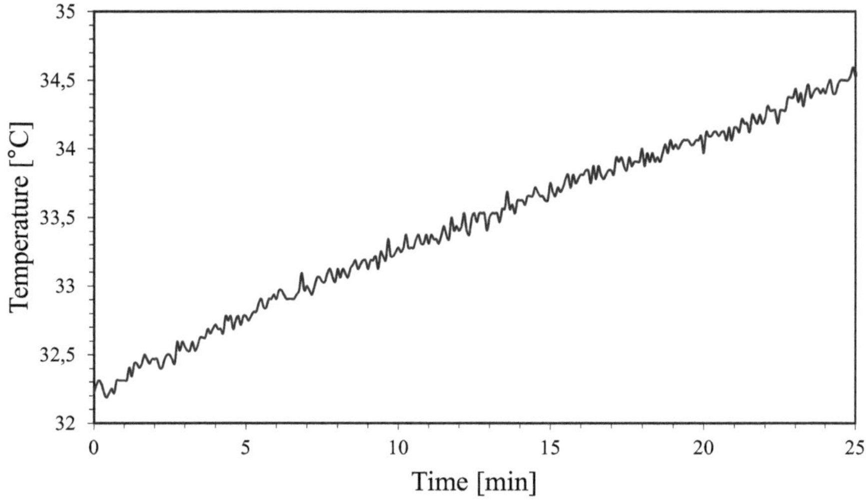

Fig. 67. Temperature data during trial 4.

The conductivity values were closer to those reported in the literature and a good signal was obtained.

In trial 5, to confirm the result of the calibration for the sweat-rate gradient, it was decided to collect sweat by placing small circular paper filters, at different times, on the volunteer's body, close to the sweat-rate sensor.

The flow depends on the amount of sweat collected by the filters, thus by weighing them it is possible to have a precise value for the sweat rate. Fig. 68 shows a low value for the capacitive gradient.

However, the Philips humidity sensor discussed in Chapter 3 showed a variation of 50% in humidity for 10 pF capacitance variation. Thus, the gradient of trial 5 showed a good behavior.

Fig. 69 shows the calibrated flow. A comparison between the sensors and the filters is shown in Fig. 70 and proves the validity of the calibration.

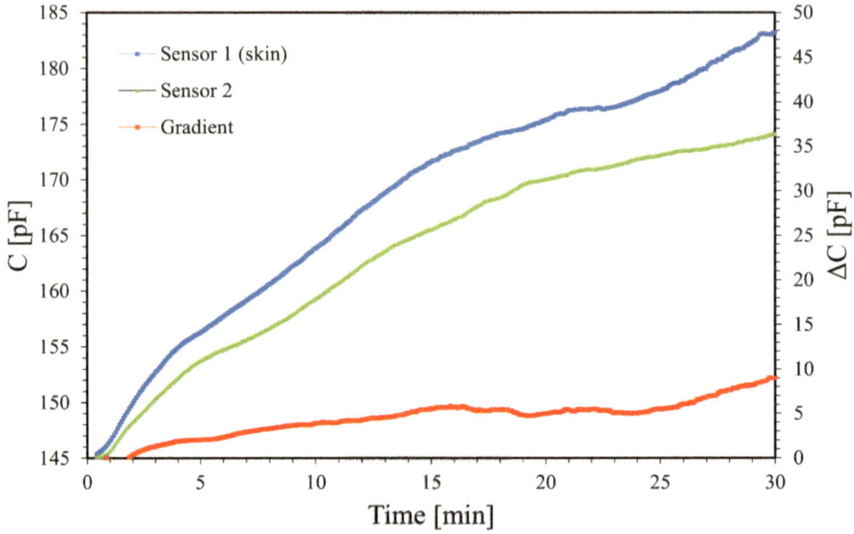

Fig. 68. Gradient of capacitances in trial 5.

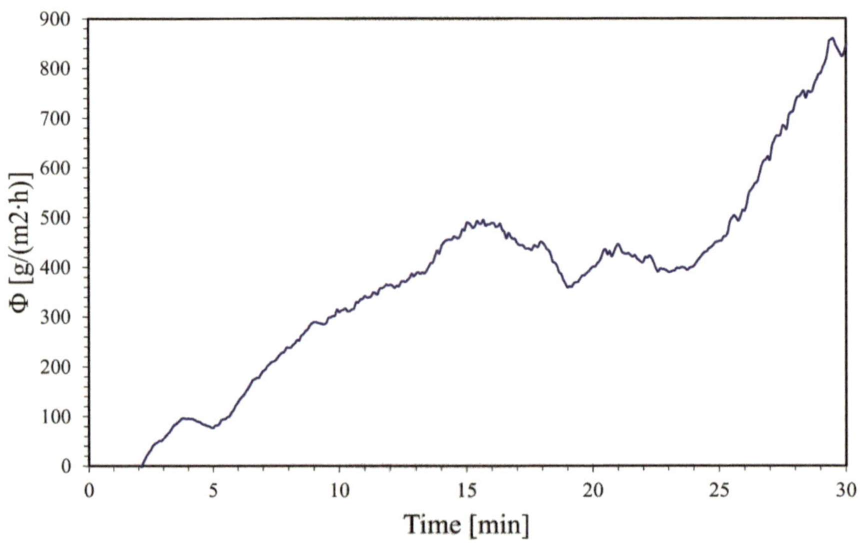

Fig. 46. Calibrated flow.

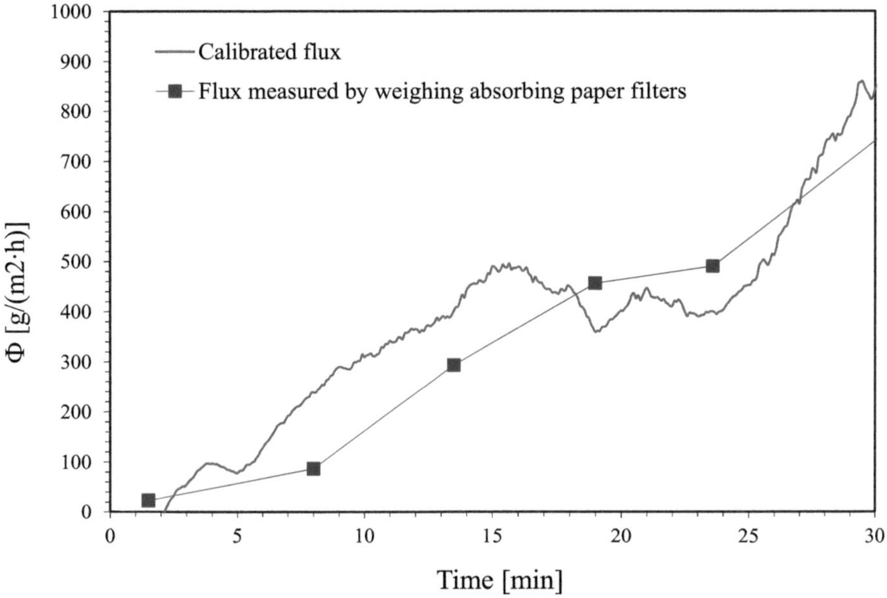

Fig. 47. Comparison between the calibrated flow and the flow measured by weighing paper filters.

Fig. 71 shows the temperature during trial 5.

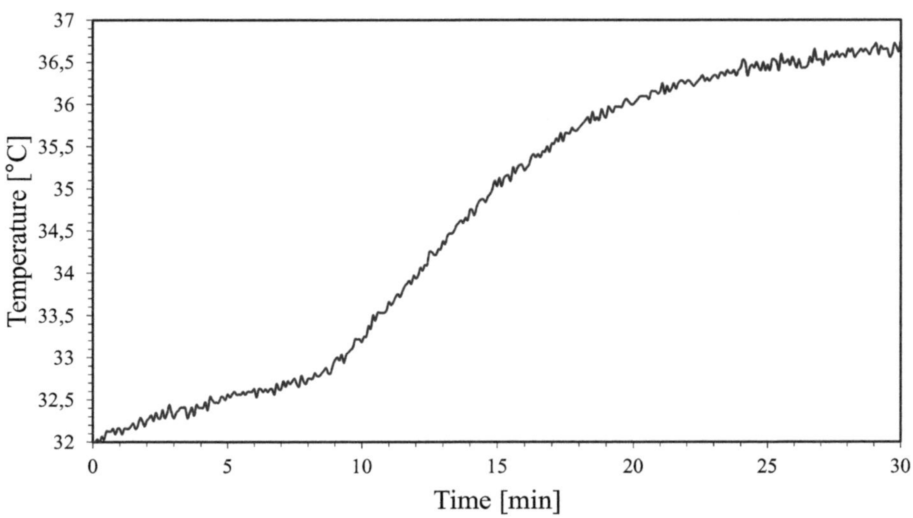

Fig. 48. Temperature data during trial 5.

4.4 Conclusions

The purpose of this book was to demonstrate that it was possible to create wearable sensors that can carry out chemical measurements on samples of biological fluids. One way to achieve this has been shown and the conductivity and sweat rate sensors represent the first step towards such sensors being fully integrated into garments.

They are small and flexible, with a reasonable cost. The conductivity (including the ADT7301) and sweat rate sensors occupy 20 mm^2 and 50 mm^2 respectively.

The individual components, and hence the overall system, are quite fragile. This is typical of early prototypes, and is not surprising given how challenging the sensors and systems are. Improvements are also needed to increase the reliability of the system.

The data gathered from exercise trials show that the textile patch operates successfully as a passive pump and can continuously deliver fresh sweat to the sensors.

However, its use in the present configuration is mainly useful with big "sweaters". Thus, efforts should be made to decrease the amount of sweat needed to make it wet.

With regard to individual measurements, performances are reasonably good. However, for the sweat rate, the humidity sensors could be improved by testing other materials with lower dielectric constants and/or better hydrophilic properties. The strong points are its simplicity, low cost, wearability, and the fact that continuous measurements can be made.

Moreover, it has been shown how the sweat-rate sensor is able to follow the variations of flow emitted by the skin with a good approximation.

The use of the sweat-rate sensor in open air may create problems if there is wind, and no tests were performed in this situation. Possible artifacts caused by movements when the device is used in different conditions from cycling need to be investigated.

The conductivity sensor provided good results in the last trial when better contact with the skin was ensured. This means that it needs to be placed better onto the pump to ensure contact with the channel and we believe that BIOTEX partners could improve sweat collection in the device. In fact, problems were experienced during the trials in terms of the quantity of sweat needed to wet the pump.

Some measurement channels in the BIOTEX device did not seem to be completely independent, which could explain part of the noise affecting the measurements. The limited possibility of visualizing data in real time sometimes meant that operators were only aware of measurement problems at the end of testing.

Testing the system has also highlighted two other issues that could represent possible directions of future work:

1. The need to allow between 10 and 20 (even 30) minutes “priming” time, before the sensors begin to work. This is the minimum time needed for the subject to produce enough sweat to wet the pump. Reducing the amount of sweat needed for the measurements and thus the priming time would represent a great improvement.
2. The effect of the flow rate on the response of the conductivity sensor.
3.

References

[1] M. J. Patterson, S. D. Galloway, M. A. Nimmo, "Variations in regional sweat composition in normal human males," Experimental Physiology, 85(6), pp. 869-875, 2000.